New Bridges 2e

Fichier de l'élève

Programme 2010

Sous la direction de François GUARY
et Marie FORT-COUDERC

par

Marie FORT-COUDERC
Professeur certifié

François GUARY
Professeur agrégé

Gaël MANESCAU
Professeur certifié

Sylvie PERSEC
Professeur agrégé

Serge TRIPODI
Professeur agrégé

Claire ZEPPILLI
Professeur agrégé

Avec la collaboration de

Patricia VRINAT-HINDLE
Professeur agrégé

Nathan

Sommaire

Sommaire

Édition : Axelle Thomas
Maquette : Patrick Deiller
Mise en page : JPMsa
Couverture : Denis Hoch

Crédits photographiques : p. 69 ht : Archives du 7e Art – Photo 12 ; **p. 69 bas** : Amnesty International ; **p. 70 ht** : DR ; **p. 70 bas** : Advertising Archives ; **p. 74** : Reents/Siemoneit/Corbis Sygma

Building bridges page 15

NEW YORK

Meet the Boutins

READING COMPREHENSION

A. True or false? Circle the correct answer and justify with keywords.

1. T F The children sleep in the family room.

....

2. T F The family doesn't like outdoor activities.

....

3. T F Stony Brook is near Long Island.

....

4. T F There is a lot to do in the village.

....

B. Write as much information as you can about each member of the family: name, age, hobby, occupation...

1. Mother: ....
2. Father: ....
3. Elder son: ....
4. Younger son: ....
5. Daughter: ....

PHONÉTIQUE – Les voyelles simples

Your CD 3-5 — CD 1 7-9

A. Classez les mots ci-dessous dans le tableau selon la prononciation de la voyelle simple en gras. (Écrivez le chiffre correspondant.) Vérifiez ensuite à l'écoute.

1. *bee* – **2.** *pig* – **3.** *hen* – **4.** *cat* – **5.** *calf* – **6.** *dog* – **7.** *horse* – **8.** *bull* – **9.** *goose* – **10.** *duck* – **11.** *bird* – **12.** *hippopotamus*

/ʊ/	/ɪ/	/æ/	/e/	/ɒ/	/ʌ/	/ə/	/ɑː/	/ɔː/	/ɜː/	/iː/	/uː/

B. Écoutez et écrivez 1 après le mot prononcé en premier et 2 après l'autre.

1. *hut:* .... / *hot:* .... – **2.** *cat:* .... / *kit:* .... – **3.** *bad:* .... / *but:* ....

4. *dog:* .... / *door:* .... – **5.** *good:* .... / *moon:* .... – **6.** *food:* .... / *book:* ....

7. *sheep:* .... / *ship:* .... – **8.** *it:* .... / *eat:* .... – **9.** *feet:* .... / *fit:* ....

10. *sick:* .... / *seek:* .... – **11.** *bud:* .... / *bed:* .... – **12.** *went:* .... / *want:* ....

C. Prononcez les mots correspondant aux transcriptions phonétiques et écrivez-les. Vérifiez ensuite à l'écoute.

1. /kəm'pliːt/ : ....
2. /'feɪməs/ : ....
3. /pə'zɪʃən/ : ....
4. /bɔːn/ : ....
5. /'kɛəlɪs/ : ....
6. /'riːzn/ : ....
7. /frend/ : ....
8. /'bʊtʃə/ : ....
9. /mætʃ/ : ....
10. /'kʌntrɪ/ : ....
11. /'dɔːtə/ : ....
12. /gɜːl/ : ....
13. /bɪ'kɒz/ : ....
14. /dɪ'sembə/ : ....
15. /ɪk'spreʃən/ : ....

NEW YORK

So much to do!

LISTENING COMPREHENSION

CD 1 / 4-6

1 Part one

A. Who is calling Tess? ....

....

B. Give two reasons for his call.

1. ....
2. ....

C. Write down the names of the places in New York the Boutins will visit with the French student.

1. .... 5. ....
2. .... 6. ....
3. .... 7. ....
4. .... 8. ....

D. What will they eat in the street? ☐ a hamburger ☐ a hot dog ☐ a pancake ☐ a doughnut

2 Part two

E. Listen to Part two twice and complete these sentences while and after listening.

1. In Stony Brook, near the ...., there's a beautiful .... which is great for ....
2. After lunch, they could go to an .... café or to a .... on the campus.
3. If they go to the ...., they'll go sailing and scuba .... The student can also .... lacrosse or play .... with the two boys.
4. The Boutins are really a .... family!

3 Part three

F. True or false? Circle the correct answer and justify with keywords.

1. T F The Boutins love to have barbecues.

....

2. T F They are vegetarians.

....

3. T F They don't eat much.

....

4. T F On Sundays, they have a small breakfast.

....

G. When and where will Tess and Andrew meet?

....

Building bridges page 17

OTTAWA

The Wilsons' house

READING COMPREHENSION

The rental agent wrote an ad for the Wilsons' house but made ten factual mistakes in the property details. Underline these mistakes and justify briefly underneath.

We strongly advise you to rent this very nice apartment in downtown Ottawa. It is quite a big place with four bedrooms which can accommodate up to eight people. The owners, who are away on holiday, welcome families with children but would rather not have any pets in their house. Handicapped people won't have any problem getting in and out of the house. Children will love the playground and enjoy the swimming pool which is just one kilometre away. You will find the washing machine, satellite TV and heating system (*chauffage*) very convenient. Local transport is rather poor, but you will find a car rental agency within walking distance. Tourist attractions are near at hand and you can practise various sports. Another important detail: the owners don't mind smokers.

1. ....
2. ....
3. ....
4. ....
5. ....
6. ....
7. ....
8. ....
9. ....
10. ....

PHONÉTIQUE – Les voyelles multiples (diphtongues)

Your CD 6-7 — CD 1 13-14

- On produit une **diphtongue** lorsque la voix glisse **d'une voyelle vers une autre voyelle**.
- Le **premier élément** d'une diphtongue est **prononcé avec plus de force** que le deuxième.
- Une diphtongue **suivie de /ə/** devient une **triphtongue** : *fire* /faɪə/ – *flower* /ˈflaʊə/.

A. Dans les mots ci-dessous les lettres en gras correspondent à des diphtongues. Écrivez chaque mot dans la colonne appropriée. Aidez-vous du tableau du rabat V si nécessaire. Vérifiez ensuite vos réponses à l'écoute.

snake – *fly* – *boy* – *goat* (chèvre) – *cow* – *deer* (cerf) – *hare* (lièvre) – *moorhen* (poule d'eau)

/aɪ/	/eɪ/	/aʊ/	/əʊ/	/ɔɪ/	/ɪə/	/ʊə/	/ɛə/
....	....	....	....	....	....	....	....

B. Lisez chaque mot à haute voix et cochez la bonne prononciation de la diphtongue en gras. Vérifiez ensuite vos réponses à l'écoute.

1. *baker*: ☐ /eɪ/ – ☐ /aɪ/
2. *cold*: ☐ /ʊə/ – ☐ /əʊ/
3. *slow*: ☐ /əʊ/ – ☐ /aʊ/
4. *great*: ☐ /ɪə/ – ☐ /eɪ/
5. *now*: ☐ /aʊ/ – ☐ /ʊə/
6. *don't*: ☐ /əʊ/ – ☐ /aʊ/
7. *danger*: ☐ /eɪ/ – ☐ /aɪ/
8. *wear*: ☐ /əʊ/ – ☐ /ɛə/
9. *sure*: ☐ /ʊə/ – ☐ /əʊ/
10. *know*: ☐ /aʊ/ – ☐ /əʊ/
11. *road*: ☐ /aʊ/ – ☐ /əʊ/
12. *either*: ☐ /eɪ/ – ☐ /aɪ/
13. *ear*: ☐ /ɪə/ – ☐ /eɪ/
14. *care*: ☐ /ɛə/ – ☐ /eɪ/
15. *fight*: ☐ /ɔɪ/ – ☐ /aɪ/

OTTAWA

Have fun...

LISTENING COMPREHENSION

CD 1 / 10-12

1 General comprehension

A. Listen to the whole dialogue and tick what Ashley wants to know.

- ☐ the various programmes
- ☐ the exact location of *Adventure Tours*
- ☐ the number of people allowed on a raft
- ☐ the equipment needed
- ☐ what happens in case of bad weather
- ☐ the safety (*sécurité*) measures
- ☐ the rates (*tarifs*)
- ☐ the length (*longueur*) of the trip

2 Part one

B. Ashley would like her friend to experience ....

C. Translate this expression: ....

D. Complete this passage while and after listening to Michael. (one blank = one word)

MICHAEL: Well, you've come to the .... place! Whitewater .... on the .... River is a lot of .... We have great .... pretty warm .... all summer long... Did you know that the Ottawa River .... through a .... of more than a .... islands? There are also nice .... , rock formations and...

3 Part two

E. True or false? Circle the correct answer and justify orally.

1. T F Ashley says that her friend is an advanced /əd'vɑːnst/ rafter.
2. T F A High Adventure Day Trip is for non-experienced /ɪk'spɪərɪənst/ rafters.
3. T F Up to ten people can fit onto (*tenir dans*) a raft.
4. T F A Gentle Raft Day Trip is not dangerous.

4 Part three

F. What clothes does Michael recommend wearing?

- ☐ low-cut running shoes
- ☐ sneakers (*baskets*)
- ☐ water shoes
- ☐ jogging suit
- ☐ shorts
- ☐ jeans
- ☐ Bermuda shorts
- ☐ bathing suit
- ☐ wool (*laine*) sweater
- ☐ cotton T-shirt
- ☐ nylon windbreaker (*coupe-vent*)
- ☐ wet suit (*combinaison*)

G. Fill in the blanks in the following passage (one blank = one word): We paddle (*pagayer*) .... or shine. We .... cancel (*annuler*) because of the ....

H. How much do the following cost?

1. Gentle Day Trip: $ ....
2. High Adventure Day Trip: $ ....

I. Write the names of the other activities mentioned by Michael and translate them.

1. ....
2. ....
3. ....

Building bridges
page 18

SYDNEY
The Aussie experience

READING COMPREHENSION

A. Why is Australia referred to as "Down Under"? When you look at the Globe, Australia sims to be

B. Use the context to deduce the meaning of "Sydneysider" (l. 3): Les gens qui habitent à Sydney

C. Find the equivalents of these words in the leaflet (in the right order).

1. *s'étendre sur :* Spread over
2. *port :* Harbour
3. *fierté :* proud
4. *innombrable :* Countless
5. *réserve naturelle :* wild life reserves
6. *en plein air :* Outdoors
7. *tourisme :* Sightseeing
8. *avoir vue sur :* over look
9. *scintillant :* glistening
10. *animé :* lively
11. *bourdonner :* buzzes
12. *plongée sous-marine :* Scuba diving
13. *plongée avec masque et tuba :* [illegible] mask an
14. *accueillir :* attracting

D. True or false? Circle the correct answer and justify with keywords.

1. T F Sydney was the first city built in Australia. True
2. T F Most Sydneysiders come from Indonesia. False
3. T F Culture has an important place in Sydney. True
4. T F It is not easy to reach Sydney's beaches. False
5. T F There is little to see outside the city centre. ....

E. What famous event was held in Sydney in 2000? ....

PHONÉTIQUE – Les consonnes

Your CD 8-10 · CD 1 19-21

A. Classez ces mots dans le tableau selon la prononciation des consonnes en gras. Aidez-vous du rabat V si nécessaire. Vérifiez ensuite vos réponses à l'écoute.

cat – thin – this – song – yes – shop – church – pleasure – page – what – hair

/ð/	/θ/	/j/	/ʃ/	/tʃ/	/k/	/ŋ/	/w/	/h/	/ʒ/	/dʒ/
....	....	....	....	....	....	....	....	....	....	....

B. Écoutez et écrivez 1 après le mot prononcé en premier et 2 après l'autre.

1. *shop:* .... / *chop:* .... – 2. *day:* .... / *they:* .... – 3. *thin:* .... / *tin:* ....
4. *both:* .... / *boat:* .... – 5. *dare:* .... / *bare:* .... – 6. *cash:* .... / *catch:* ....
7. *right:* .... / *might:* .... – 8. *van:* .... / *ban:* .... – 9. *heart:* .... / *art:* ....
10. *eye:* .... / *high:* .... – 11. *sing:* .... / *sin:* .... – 12. *wet:* .... / *vet:* ....
13. *ferry:* .... / *very:* .... – 14. *beat:* .... / *Pete:* .... – 15. *sheep:* .... / *cheap:* ....

C. Prononcez les mots suivants et écrivez-les. Vérifiez ensuite à l'écoute.

1. /saɪˈkɒlədʒɪ/ : ....
2. /ˈeksəsaɪz/ : ....
3. /ˈnɒlɪdʒ/ : ....
4. /ˈdʒaɪənt/ : ....
5. /ˈfəʊtəgræf/ : ....
6. /ˈæktjʊəlɪ/ : ....
7. /ˈmeʒə/ : ....
8. /ˈæθliːt/ : ....
9. /huːz/ : ....

SYDNEY

Meet the Jacksons

LISTENING COMPREHENSION

CD 1 / 15-18

1 Part one

A. Complete the grid with keywords while and after listening to Shirley and Tony.

	Why did the Jacksons choose to live in Kirribilli?
Shirley	....
Tony	....

2 Part two

B. Tick the correct sentences while and after listening to Charlene. Justify orally.

- ☐ She loves having a big garden.
- ☐ Charlene's kangaroo loves the garden too.
- ☐ She enjoys swimming in the ocean.
- ☐ They have palm trees and exotic plants.
- ☐ She loves to hear birds sing all day long.
- ☐ She usually goes to school on a ferry.
- ☐ Their house is a typical Australian house.
- ☐ She cannot get used to Australian food.
- ☐ The view from the front porch is fantastic.
- ☐ She can watch sailing boats.

3 Part three

C. True or false? Circle the correct answer and justify orally.

1. T F On Sundays the Jacksons usually stay at home or visit relatives.
2. T F The Jacksons often go shopping in downtown Sydney.
3. T F Bondi beach is the ideal place for surfing.
4. T F Charlene loves going to the beach in July or August.
5. T F The Jacksons enjoy walking in the bush every morning.

4 Part four

D. Complete this passage while and after listening to Shirley. (one blank = one word)

I .... in the Old Sydney .... in .... Sydney. That's near the Royal Botanic .... And I meet some .... friends of mine every Friday .... , and well... we .... talk about... well... about .... Sometimes we go to a .... nearby. Oh, we love to .... like real .... I mean... I think after so many .... in Australia, well... we almost are ....

GRAMMAIRE
Rappels

1 Présent simple et présent *BE+ING*

A. Mettez les énoncés à la forme négative (–) ou interrogative (?).

1. (–) *Alan attends my classes.* ....
2. (–) *Dorothy has a new mobile.* ....
3. (?) *Harry does as well as his classmates.* ....
4. (?) *They often mock him.* ....
5. (?) *They're having lunch now.* ....
6. (–) *I'm feeling very well today.* ....

B. Mettez le verbe entre parenthèses au présent simple ou au présent *BE+ING*.

INTERVIEWER: (you – often – read) .... fiction?
NATASHA: (I – read) .... all sorts of books. My favourite book is Lord of the Rings. (I – love) .... the way (Tolkien – write) .... It's not related to what (I – do) .... right now, so it's nice to go into a different world.
INTERVIEWER: (you – keep) .... a diary at the moment?
NATASHA: (I – keep – usually) .... a journal. But at the present time (I – write) .... a book about my life.

2 Prétérit simple

C. Mettez les énoncés à la forme négative (–) ou interrogative (?).

1. (?) *The journalists found out who the leader was.*
....
2. (–) *They did what they were supposed to do.*
....
3. (?) *They brought the prisoners food and medicine.*
....
4. (–) *They knew what to think.*
....

3 Formes du verbe après un auxiliaire

D. Mettez le verbe entre parenthèses à la forme qui convient.

1. *I'm afraid he is still (wait) .... for us outside the building.*
2. *As far as I know, he has never (be) .... (arrest) .... before.*
3. *Did you (recognize) .... the man you had (see) .... the day before?*
4. *The building was probably (build) .... after World War II.*
5. *He was (dream) .... of buying the latest computer screen.*

4 Interrogation

E. Aidez-vous des réponses pour compléter chaque question avec un des mots interrogatifs suivants et mettez les verbes à la forme voulue : *WHEN, HOW MANY, HOW LONG, HOW OLD*.

1. *QUESTION: (you – get) the idea for Harry Potter?* ....
   ANSWER: In the 90s. I was in the train and the idea just came to me.
2. *QUESTION: (it – take) to write the first book?* ....
   ANSWER: Five years, although during that time I was also planning parts of the sequels.
3. *QUESTION: (Harry Potter – be)?* ....
   ANSWER: In book one he is 11, and he is one year older in each subsequent book.
4. *QUESTION: (books – be sold)?* ....
   ANSWER: More than 100 million copies have been sold so far, in 42 different languages.

5 Possession

F. Remplacez le pronom entre parenthèses par l'adjectif possessif (*MY, YOUR*, etc.) ou le pronom possessif (*MINE, YOURS*, etc.) correspondant.

1. *That's (he)* .... *car, not (you)* .... *!*
2. *I think it was (I)* .... *idea, not (she)* ....
3. *Don't you think it's (we)* .... *problem, not (they)* .... *?*
4. *That's (she)* .... *bag, not (we)* ....

G. Formez un génitif avec les éléments en gras.

1. *Is this* ***the car that belongs to your parents?*** ....
2. *I don't like* ***the new film of Jonathan Lee.*** ....
3. ***The new boyfriend of Clare*** *speaks Chinese.* ....
4. ***The population of the world*** *is increasing.* ....

6 Pronoms personnels

H. Remplacez le(s) mot(s) entre parenthèses par le pronom personnel complément correspondant.

1. *Edith never allowed (we)* .... *to read the letters Sean had sent (she)* ....
2. *She sent (I)* .... *her book but she didn't send (her book)* .... *to (George)* ....
3. *I asked (they)* .... *to tell (you)* .... *where they were.*

7 Comparatif des adjectifs

I. Mettez l'adjectif entre parenthèses à la forme qui convient : (+) comparatif de supériorité, (–) comparatif d'infériorité, (=) comparatif d'égalité. Ajoutez *THAN* ou *AS* selon le cas.

1. *Your cousin is (–) (optimistic) ... you, isn't he?* ....
2. *He doesn't think his life will be (+) (hard) ... his parents'.* ....
3. *It was far (+) (difficult) ... I had expected.* ....
4. *His driving is (+) (bad) ... his brother's.* ....
5. *He wants a (+) (good) world ... today's.* ....
6. *It was not (= important) ... you thought, was it?* ....

LISTENERS' CORNER
My greatest challenge

LISTENING COMPREHENSION

CD 1/ P3-24

1 Get ready

A. Before listening to the interview, read these place-names aloud and tick those which correspond to American states.

1. ☐ San Francisco /ˌsænfræn'sɪskəʊ/
2. ☐ Connecticut /kə'netɪkət/
3. ☐ Nebraska /nɪ'bræskə/
4. ☐ New York /njuː'jɔːk/
5. ☐ Ohio /əʊ'haɪəʊ/
6. ☐ Bristol /'brɪstəl/
7. ☐ Indiana /ˌɪndɪ'ænə/
8. ☐ Hartford /'hɑːtfəd/
9. ☐ Lincoln /'lɪŋkən/
10. ☐ Pennsylvania /ˌpensɪl'veɪnɪə/
11. ☐ Missouri /mɪ'zʊərɪ/
12. ☐ Illinois /ˌɪlɪ'nɔɪ/

2 Part one

B. Which of these two identity cards is Lindsay's?

	Place of birth	Town and state of residence	Age / Occupation
1	Unknown	Bristol / Connecticut	25 / student in sociology
2	Bristol	Hartford / Connecticut	27 / student in psychology

C. True or false? Circle the correct answer and justify.

1. T F Lindsey joined the *Togetherness* program six months ago. ....
2. T F The program lasted six months. ....
3. T F The participants report their experience in a TV interview. ....
4. T F Lindsey's walk took place in autumn and winter. ....

D. Lindsey walked from .... to .... She crossed .... states.

3 Part two

E. How many miles did Lindsey walk? ....

F. Listen to this passage twice and fill in the blanks while and after listening. (one blank = one word)

Lindsey: I sometimes .... out in the open. I spent time with complete .... But all in all I reckon I .... to adjust to different .... and ways of life. I stayed with all sorts of people. I even met a South African family in a remote .... in ....

G. True or false? Circle the correct answer and justify.

1. T F Lindsey found it easy to cover such long distances.
....

2. T F Lindsey doesn't regret her tiring journey.
....

3. T F Lindsey has lost contact with the people she met.
....

4. T F This experience has changed Lindsey's life.
....

TEXT 1

Alone in Alaska

READING COMPREHENSION

A. Why was Alex standing in the snow beside the road?

☐ He was waiting for the bus. ☐ He was lost.

☐ He was waiting for a car to stop. ☐ He was waiting for a friend.

B. Deduce the meaning of "hitchhiker" (l. 2): ....

C. Fill in the grid with information about Alex.

Age	....
Origin / Destination	....
Reason for leaving	....

D. Quote keywords showing that Jim thinks Alex is not well equipped to face the cold.

....

E. How did Jim Gallien try to help Alex? Quote four elements.

1. .... 3. ....

2. .... 4. ....

F. Which adjectives best define Alex in this passage?

shy – determined – lost – impatient – adventurous – rude (*impoli*) – independent – cheerful (*joyeux*)

G. Why did Alex give Jim his comb, his money and his watch?

☐ Jim needed them. ☐ Jim had asked him to do so. ☐ Alex did not need them anymore.

PRATIQUER LA GRAMMAIRE

Pronoms personnels et possessifs → Précis grammatical 23

H. Complétez avec *him, her, his, hers, himself* ou *herself*.

1. *Alex said he wanted to enjoy* ....
2. *Mary said that a good friend of* .... *was living there.*
3. *Alice sat down and tried to make* .... *comfortable.*
4. *Sarah said to Jim that she was 19 and she showed* .... *passport.*
5. *Jim was thinking about* .... *wife who was waiting for* .... *at home.*

I. Traduisez en utilisant les possessifs qui conviennent.

1. J'ai pris leurs sacs, pas le tien.

....

2. Cette voiture est à moi. La leur est dans notre garage.

....

TEXT 2

The expedition

READING COMPREHENSION

1 Part one

A. Who is who? Match each character with one (or two) element(s) in the second column:

Professor Challenger •	• the narrator
Professor Summerlee •	• a journalist
Edward Dunn Malone •	• a scientist
Lord John Roxton •	• an adventurer
	• the professor who suggests the expedition

B. What is the goal of the expedition?

....

C. Who do the underlined pronouns refer to?

1. In front of me there was another man standing. (l. 11): ....
2. I've already been up the Amazon. (l. 13): ....
3. We'll be companions on this adventure. (l. 19): ....

D. Why does Professor Challenger think that Lord Roxton will be perfect for the expedition? (Quote.)

....

E. Quote the sentence indicating that the expedition might be dangerous.

....

F. True or false?

T F We don't learn anything else about Professor Challenger's discovery.

2 Part two

G. Quote the elements indicating that Lord Roxton is:

1. a hunter and traveller

....

2. welcoming

....

3. enthusiastic about the location of the expedition

....

4. optimistic about the discovery

....

H. Read the passage from "Once you know it..." (l. 25) to "... to discover it" (l. 28). What can we deduce about Professor Challenger's discovery? Justify with keywords.

The discovery must be:

☐ extraordinary ☐ minor ☐ common ☐ unexpected (*inattendu*) ☐ exciting

....

....

I. The last paragraph implies that the explorers (several answers):

- ☐ will read Professor Challenger's instructions during their voyage at sea.
- ☐ are free to do whatever they want when they reach their destination.
- ☐ will have to conform to Professor Challenger's wishes.
- ☐ will have to wait until they arrive before they can read Professor Challenger's instructions.

Ten words to remember

Find the equivalents of these ten words in the text (in the right order) and learn them by heart.

1. *partir en expédition :* ....
2. *découverte :* ....
3. *célèbre :* ....
4. *scientifique* (nom) *:* ....
5. *région :* ....
6. *voyageur :* ....
7. *sauvage :* ....
8. *carte :* ....
9. *couler* (fleuve ou rivière) *:* ....
10. *crier :* ....

ENRICHIR SON LEXIQUE – Le voyage

Mardi 3.

Classez ces mots et expressions dans le tableau ci-dessous. Certains mots peuvent se trouver dans plusieurs colonnes.

Nouns: *coach – ID card – cruise – travel agency – railway station – baggage / luggage – crossing – landing – domestic flight – sleeping car – voyage – stop-over – boarding card – harbour – check-in desk – baggage claim – platform – journey – quay – customs – trip – left-luggage – connecting flight*

Verbs: *land – go aboard – take off – hitch-hike – pack – unpack – board / get on – get off – travel – sail*

Air	*Nouns:* .... *Verbs:* ....
Sea	*Nouns:* Cruise .... *Verbs:* ....
Road	*Nouns:* coach .... *Verbs:* ....
Rail	*Nouns:* .... *Verbs:* ....
General	*Nouns:* ID card .... *Verbs:* ....

PRATIQUER LA GRAMMAIRE

1 Le *PRESENT PERFECT* → Précis grammatical 5, 6

A. Soulignez les formes verbales au *present perfect* et entourez celles au prétérit. Répondez ensuite aux questions a et b.

1. *"I've already been up the Amazon. I know the area well."* (l. 13)
2. *"I've seen it all. I think it's the most wonderful place on this planet."* (l. 24)
3. *I first went to South America twenty years ago.*

a. Quelle autre forme verbale trouve-t-on associée au *present perfect* : □ le présent ou □ le prétérit ?

b. Relevez les expressions de temps associées au prétérit et indiquez si elles expriment un lien ou bien une rupture avec le présent : ....

B. Mettez les verbes entre parenthèses au *present perfect* ou au prétérit.

1. *He (give) me all the information I need!* ....
2. *We (accept) their proposal last week.* ....
3. *They (write) that letter on Tuesday.* ....
4. *(you / see) him last night?* ....
5. *I (live) here all my life. I know the place very well.* ....

2 *SOMETHING, ANYTHING, NOTHING* → Précis grammatical 23E

C. Justifiez l'emploi de *ANYTHING* dans les énoncés ci-dessous à l'aide de l'une des trois propositions suivantes :

a. Il s'agit d'une question. **b.** *Anything* est précédé d'une forme négative.

c. *Anything* signifie « tout » ou « n'importe quoi ».

1. *"Once you know it, you'll understand that anything is possible – anything."* (l. 25) ....
2. *Don't ask him anything!* ....
3. *Is there anything else?* ....

D. Complétez avec *SOMETHING*, *ANYTHING* ou *NOTHING*.

1. *I haven't found* .... *interesting to read.*
2. *Give me* .... *to drink! I'm terribly thirsty.*
3. *"What can I buy him for his birthday?"*
   "I am sure he'll be happy with ....*!"*
4. *It's too late. There is* .... *we can do about it.*

3 Prépositions et expressions du mouvement

E. Traduisez les passages donnés en vous attachant tout particulièrement aux mouvements exprimés par les prépositions soulignées. Ajoutez des verbes supplémentaires en français si nécessaire.

1. *"I walked out of the hall into the night."* (l. 17)

....

2. *"It was full of strange objects from around the world."* (l. 21)

....

3. *"The Amazon River flows through a forest (...)."* (l. 26)

....

CHECK YOUR SKILLS

COMPRÉHENSION DE L'ÉCRIT

Comprendre un article de presse

1. **This article is about a young man who**
 ☐ took part in a sailing competition. ☐ sailed around the world by himself.
2. **Complete the following information about Mike. (one blank = one word)**
 a. Mike's age when he started his voyage: ...., when he returned: ....
 b. He left on (give dates): ....; he returned in ....
3. **Use the context to deduce the meaning of:**
 a. cheering (l. 1): ☐ *huer* ☐ *rire* ☐ *acclamer*
 b. overwhelmed (l. 7-l. 9): ☐ *en colère* ☐ *triste* ☐ *bouleversé*
 c. be close to tears (l. 8): ☐ *être en larmes* ☐ *être au bord des larmes* ☐ *refuser de pleurer*
4. **What difficulties did Mike face during his voyage? (several answers)**
 ☐ storms ☐ sharks (*requins*) ☐ adapting his route ☐ low spirits (*moral*) ☐ diseases
5. **When Mike returned home, people**
 ☐ were indifferent. ☐ were welcoming and supportive. ☐ thought he was crazy.
6. **In the future, Mike** ☐ will never embark on such an adventure again.
 ☐ will envisage other adventures but only at sea. ☐ may also consider adventures on land.

Je me situe par rapport au CECRL

Questions	Quand je lis cet extrait, je peux :		☺	😐	☹
1	en reconnaître le sujet principal.	A2			
2	y trouver des informations précises.	A2			
3	deviner, à l'aide du contexte, le sens de certains mots inconnus.	B1			
4	en reconnaître les points significatifs.	B1			
5-6	comprendre les descriptions de sentiments ou de souhaits.	B1			

INTERACTION ORALE

Prendre part à une interview

Je me situe par rapport au CECRL

Quand je prends part à cette interview, je peux :		☺	😐	☹
poser des questions simples portant sur des thèmes familiers.	A2			
dire comment je me sens et exprimer mes sentiments.	A2			
demander de répéter en termes simples quand je ne comprends pas.	A2			
interviewer quelqu'un sur un sujet précis si j'ai préparé le questionnaire ; je peux également poser des questions spontanées.	B1			
participer activement et sans préparation à une discussion sur un thème qui m'est familier, même si je dois parfois chercher mes mots.	B1			
prendre l'initiative dans une conversation.	B1			

LISTENERS' CORNER
The voice

LISTENING COMPREHENSION

CD 1 34-35

1 Get ready

A. Before listening to the story, use the definitions to translate the following words.

1. widow /ˈwɪdəʊ/: a woman whose husband has died. ....
2. nephew /ˈnefjuː/: the son of your brother or sister. ....
3. wireless /ˈwaɪəlɪs/: old-fashioned word meaning "radio". ....
4. eerie /ˈɪərɪ/: strange and frightening. ....
5. cease /siːs/: stop. ....
6. buzzing noise: a continuous sound, like that of a bee (*abeille*). ....

2 Part one

B. True or false? Circle the correct answer and justify by quoting keywords.

T F Mrs Mary Harter was a poor young married woman.

....

C. Charles was: ☐ Mrs Harter's uncle. ☐ Mrs Harter's nephew. ☐ Mrs Harter's husband.

D. Fill in each blank. (one blank = one word)

1. Charles had convinced Mrs Harter to buy a .... to keep her ....
2. Three months later, the first .... thing happened.

E. Where was Charles that night?

☐ at a birthday party. ☐ at a bridge party. ☐ at a concert.

F. What programme was on the radio that evening? ....

G. What happened while Mrs Harter was listening to the radio? (several answers)

☐ Annie Laurie started crying.
☐ Mrs Harter heard buzzing sounds.
☐ The music stopped suddenly.
☐ Charles came back home.

3 Part two

H. True or false? Circle the correct answer and justify by quoting keywords.

T F Mrs Harter heard a man's voice, but it was not very clear. ....

I. Whose voice did Mrs Harter hear? ....

J. What did the voice say? Fill in each blank. (one blank = one word)

"I am .... for you soon. You will be .... won't you, Mary?"

K. Tick the statements that correspond to the story.

☐ Mrs Harter jumped out of her chair.
☐ She believed she had gone to sleep for a minute or two.
☐ She turned off the wireless.
☐ She recognized the voice immediately.
☐ She thought she had had a hallucination.
☐ She thought she had been dreaming.

TEXT 1

Big money

READING COMPREHENSION

A. Who are the main characters? ....

B. Who is the narrator? ....

C. Where does the story take place? ....

From the beginning to l. 18

D. Use the context to tick the correct translations of the following words.

1. dip (l. 3): ☐ *sortir* ☐ *plonger* ☐ *enlever* ☐ *effleurer*
2. come in with sb (l. 16): ☐ *marcher avec qqn* ☐ *entrer avec qqn* ☐ *trahir qqn* ☐ *sauver qqn*

E. Della wants Johnny to: (several answers)

☐ tell the police about Paul's death. ☐ tell the police he killed Paul.
☐ become her accomplice. ☐ keep his mouth shut.

F. If Johnny doesn't do what Stella says, what will she do? ....

G. How will she do this? ....

From l. 19 to the end

H. Who are "they" in the sentences: "They've got to think it was you who died in the car." (l. 24), "They know me in Pelotta. They'll identify me." (l. 26)? ....

I. What does Della want Johnny to do now?

☐ hide Paul's body. ☐ exchange his clothes for Paul's.
☐ set fire to Paul's car. ☐ make the police believe he died in the car.

J. Use the context to deduce the meaning of "get rid of you" (l. 31): ....

PRATIQUER LA GRAMMAIRE

L'impératif → Précis grammatical 32

K. Transformez les énoncés suivants en énoncés à l'impératif.

1. *You've got to stay where you are.* ....
2. *Why don't we talk it over?* ....
3. *You mustn't talk to anyone.* ....
4. *We mustn't argue about it.* ....
5. *I want you to put the body back in the car.* ....

L. Traduisez.

1. Ne dis rien ! ....
2. Essayons de trouver une solution. ....
3. Mets ton manteau. ....
4. N'oublions pas de fermer la porte à clé. ....

TEXT 2

Suspicion

READING COMPREHENSION

1 Part one

A. Write down the names of the characters.

1. the victim: ....
2. the victim's mother: ....
3. the victim's father: ....
4. the victim's husband: ....
5. the first detective: ....
6. the second detective: ....

B. What happened to Elizabeth eight years ago? ....

C. The two detectives want to know if (several answers):

☐ Elizabeth was a violent woman.
☐ Dr. Beck was a violent man.
☐ Elizabeth and her husband were a happy couple.
☐ Kim and Hoyt Parker are a happy couple.

D. What do we learn about the relationship between Dr. Beck and his wife? (Quote.)

....

....

E. Deduce the meaning of "close" (l. 5): ☐ *fermé* ☐ *proche* ☐ *agressif*

F. Use the context to find one verb meaning *battre*: .... **. Deduce the meaning of "wife beater" (l. 17):** ☐ *Un homme qui bat sa femme.* ☐ *Une femme qui bat son mari.*

G. Use the context to tick the correct translations of the following words.

1. profess (l. 17): ☐ *enseigner* ☐ *progresser* ☐ *prétendre* ☐ *nier*
2. disturbing (l. 21): ☐ *ennuyeux* ☐ *troublant* ☐ *ridicule* ☐ *amusant*
3. hand (l. 22): ☐ *serrer la main* ☐ *tendre* ☐ *lancer* ☐ *cacher*

H. What does Carlson do at the end of Part one? What for? ....

....

....

2 Part two

I. Quote two sentences indicating that the Parkers did not expect to see such photos:

....

....

J. How did Mrs Parker know about Elizabeth's bruises?

....

K. Quote two reasons why Elizabeth's explanation for her bruises couldn't be true.

1. ....

....

2. ....

....

L. Why does Hoyt ask his wife to leave the room? (several answers)

Because he has understood that the detectives :

☐ are going to accuse him of hiding the truth.
☐ have something terrible to reveal.
☐ are sure that Dr Beck beat his wife.
☐ believe that his wife is guilty of something.

M. The detectives are convinced that ....

....

Ten words to remember

Find the equivalents of these ten words and expressions in the text (in the right order) and learn them by heart.

1. *relation :* ....
2. *proche :* ....
3. *battre* (2 verbs) *:* ....
4. *troublant :* ....
5. *tendre* (verb) *:* ....
6. *calmement :* ....
7. *signaler :* ....
8. *vérifier :* ....
9. *dossier :* ....
10. *ça t'ennuie si... ? :* ....

ENRICHIR SON LEXIQUE – Crimes et châtiments

A. Servez-vous du contexte et de votre logique pour traduire ces phrases en français.

1. *The judge said it was a very serious crime, and sentenced her to sixteen years in prison.*

....

....

2. *The defendant has a right to a fair trial.*

....

3. *58% of prisoners are in jail for non violent crimes.*

....

4. *If he is convicted, the judge may give him the death penalty.*

....

5. *He escaped in October 1938 and took refuge in Britain.*

....

6. *Jurors were unable to reach a verdict after deliberating four hours.*

....

B. Barrez la phrase qui vous paraît illogique dans chacun des paragraphes suivants.

1. *<u>Questions suspected criminals may ask:</u>* **a.** *Have I done something wrong?* – **b.** *Does this belong to you?* – **c.** *Can I call a lawyer?* – **d.** *Where are you taking me?* – **e.** *Can I make a phone call?*
2. *<u>Questions police may ask a suspected criminal:</u>* **a.** *Are you carrying any illegal drugs?* – **b.** *What are my rights?* – **c.** *Whose car is this?* – **d.** *Where were you at eight last night?*
3. *<u>Informing someone of laws and police procedures:</u>* **a.** *You are under arrest.* – **b.** *Put your hands on your head.* – **c.** *I am taking you to the police station.* – **d.** *You will have to pay a fine for this.* – **e.** *I will give you a warning this time.* – **f.** *I'm going to write a letter to your Mum.*

PRATIQUER LA GRAMMAIRE

1 *SAY* et *TELL* → Précis grammatical 42D

A. Complétez avec *SAY* ou *TELL* au prétérit.

1. *I* .... *them that we were very close.*
2. *She* .... *to him that there were no problems at all.*
3. *Carlson* .... *that he wanted to show her some photographs.*
4. *She* .... *to the policemen that she had been in a state of shock.*
5. *He* .... *her how sorry he was.*

B. Traduisez avec *SAY* ou *TELL* à la forme qui convient.

1. Ils m'ont dit que c'était trop tard mais je n'ai rien dit. ....

....

2. « Mon mari ne vous a pas dit où il était, » dit-elle. ....

....

2 *NO, NONE, NO ONE* → Précis grammatical 22C

A. Indiquez pour chacun des passages en gras s'il s'agit d'un : a. pronom désignant une personne indéfinie. **b.** pronom indiquant une quantité nulle. **c.** déterminant (placé devant un nom).

Cochez la case correspondante puis traduisez.

1. *"**No** problems?"* (l. 6) a ☐ b ☐ c ☐ : ....
2. *"No," she said. "**None**"* (l. 7) a ☐ b ☐ c ☐ : ....
3. *"**No one** hit my daughter."* (l. 12) a ☐ b ☐ c ☐ : ....

B. Traduisez à l'aide de *NO*, *NONE* ou *NO ONE*.

1. Personne ne l'a vue. ....
2. Il n'y a pas eu de victimes. ....
3. Je leur ai demandé de m'envoyer des nouvelles mais je n'en ai reçu aucune.

....

3 *NEVER* et *EVER* → Précis grammatical 28

A. Justifiez chaque emploi de *EVER* et *NEVER* à l'aide de l'une de ces propositions :

a. s'emploie dans une question. **b.** s'emploie après un superlatif. **c.** exprime une négation.

Cochez la case correspondante.

1. *"...did Dr. Beck **ever** hit your daughter?"* (l. 11) a ☐ b ☐ c ☐
2. *"He **never** hit her."* (l. 18) a ☐ b ☐ c ☐
3. *It's the best idea you've **ever** had.* a ☐ b ☐ c ☐

B. Traduisez.

1. C'est la plus grande ville que j'aie jamais visitée.

....

2. « – Êtes-vous déjà allé en Australie ? – Non, je n'y suis jamais allé. »

....

CHECK YOUR SKILLS

COMPRÉHENSION DE L'ÉCRIT

Comprendre un extrait de roman

1. **Inspector Gregson writes a letter to Sherlock Holmes to:**
   □ tell him that a murder has been committed. □ ask him for advice (*conseils*).
   □ ask him if he knows who the victim is. □ tell him that he doesn't understand what happened.
2. **Who discovered the body of the gentleman? Justify your answer:**
   □ a neighbour. □ a policeman. □ Inspector Gregson. ....
3. **What do we learn about: a.** the time of the murder? ....
   b. the victim's social class? ....
4. **"something was amiss" (l. 5) means:** □ Things were missing. □ There was something wrong.
5. **Find three elements indicating that, according to the Inspector, E.J. Drebber was not the victim of a thief (*voleur*).**
   a. .... **b.** .... **c.** ....
6. **Why does Inspector Gregson say: "the whole affair is a puzzler"? (l. 12) Quote the text.**
   a. .... **b.** ....
7. **True or false? Circle the correct answer and justify.**
   a. T F The scene of the crime has remained untouched. ....
   b. T F Inspector Gregson has given Sherlock Holmes all the information he has.
   ....

Je me situe par rapport au CECRL

Questions	Quand je lis cet extrait de roman, je peux :		☺	😐	☹
1	identifier l'information principale.	A2			
3	trouver une information particulière.	A2			
2-4	deviner, à l'aide du contexte, le sens des mots inconnus.	B1			
5-6-7	comprendre l'essentiel de la narration.	B1			

EXPRESSION ÉCRITE

Écrire une histoire

Je me situe par rapport au CECRL

Quand j'écris cette histoire, je peux :		☺	😐	☹
décrire les événements avec des phrases simples.	A2			
relier des phrases avec des mots simples tels que *and*, *then* ou *because*.	A2			
raconter une histoire en mettant en relief la succession et la cohérence des évènements et des comportements.	B1			
supprimer en me relisant les erreurs de langue les plus importantes.	B1			

LISTENERS' CORNER
The earth from space

LISTENING COMPREHENSION

1 Part one

A. Marc Garneau has travelled in space: ☐ twice ☐ three times ☐ four times.

B. In which year did his first space flight take place? ....

C. Complete the following passage with Garneau's words.

When you're down on earth, you live in a world that you can .... You can see in a ....– kilometer circle around you.

When you're up in space, you see a .... kilometers ahead of you. Your sense of .... is changed. It takes you an .... to go round the planet.

D. What did Garneau's space flights make him realize? ....

....

2 Part two

E. What does deforestation cause? Quote two elements.

1. .... 2. ....

F. Complete the following grid.

	Geographic area	Continent	Environmental problem
/ˌæməˈzəʊnɪə/	....		forced fires in the ....
/ˈbrɪtɪʃ kəˈlʌmbɪə/	....		clear cutting (*abattage*)
/ˌkælɪˈfɔːnɪə/	....		....
/ˌmedɪtəˈreɪnɪən ˈbeɪsn/	....		....
/siː əv ərˈæl/	Sea of Aral	....	a basket case (*un cas désespéré*)
/leik tʃæd/	....	....	It shrinks (*rétrécit*).

G. Complete this passage.

All these environmental problems are due to .... -produced activity. They are examples of how .... can totally ruin something.

H. What was the turning point in Marc Garneau's life?

....

I. Why aren't Canadians really aware of all these problems?

....

TEXT 1

Climate change

READING COMPREHENSION

A. Emma and Gloria are "two young activists" (*militantes*). Read the whole text and find another noun with the same meaning: ....

B. Use the context to guess the translation of the following words:

1. from overseas (l. 5): ☐ *de la mer* ☐ *des océans* ☐ *de l'étranger*
2. wide (l. 6): ☐ *sauvage* ☐ *grande* ☐ *minuscule*
3. diet (l. 8): ☐ *climat* ☐ *alimentation* ☐ *habitudes*
4. hit (l. 9): ☐ *blesser* ☐ *toucher* ☐ *cogner*
5. deal with (l. 12): ☐ *négocier* ☐ *s'attaquer au problème* ☐ *accepter*

C. What do the following pronouns refer to?

1. we (l. 3): ☐ young people ☐ British people ☐ people from overseas
2. we (l. 5): ☐ young people ☐ British people ☐ people from overseas
3. they (l. 5): ☐ young people ☐ British people ☐ people from overseas

D. Tick the sentence which corresponds neither to Emma's nor to Gloria's opinions:

☐ Young people should feel concerned about the planet's future.
☐ Gloria thinks that natural disasters will certainly cause a change in our eating habits.
☐ Natural catastrophes can often be linked (*liées*) to climate change.
☐ According to Emma the poor will be the first victims of climate change.
☐ Politicians should impose a stricter environmental policy.
☐ Young people should understand that only politicians can make people change their attitudes.

PRATIQUER LA GRAMMAIRE

Les articles *the* et ø → Précis grammatical 21

E. Complétez avec *the* ou ø.

1. .... *air and* .... *water are necessary for* .... *life on this planet.*
2. *I've tested* .... *water in this river.*
3. .... *air we breathe is polluted.*
4. .... *climate change could destroy* .... *Earth.*
5. *These are* .... *changes that we all need.*
6. *No attempt to protect* .... *environment will be successful in* .... *long run.*
7. .... *environmentalists often put* .... *blame on us.*
8. .... *man has* .... *power to affect* .... *future of our planet.*
9. .... *natural disasters will affect* .... *daily lives of our children.*

Dear diary,

READING COMPREHENSION

1 Throughout the text

A. Laura uses colloquial language (*langage familier*). Write the following words in formal English:

1. wanna (l. 8): ....
2. gonna (l. 9 - l. 15): ....
3. cos (l. 9 - l. 27): ....
4. the Gov (l. 13): ....
5. thru (l. 30): ....
6. yer stooped cow (l. 35): ....

B. Focus on phrasal verbs (*verbes à particule*).

1. Use the word in bold letters (*en gras*) and the context to complete the translation of the following verbs.

a. cut **back** (l. 15): .... *l'utilisation*
b. fade **away** (l. 23): .... *en s'effaçant*
c. leap **on** (l. 29): .... *d'un bond*
d. look **up** (l. 31): .... *les yeux*

2. Use the context to match each verb with its French equivalent:

expédier – faire marche arrière – consommer entièrement – calculer – racheter – retarder

a. work out (l. 4): ....
b. ship over (l. 8): ....
c. buy up (l. 12): ....
d. back down (l. 13): ....
e. use up (l. 23): ....
f. hold up (l. 35): ....

2 Part one

C. Use the context to guess the translation of the following words:

1. actually (l. 5): ☐ *réellement* ☐ *actuellement* ☐ *habituellement*
2. heating (l. 6 – l. 16): ☐ *chaleur* ☐ *transport* ☐ *chauffage*
3. riot (l. 12): ☐ *élection* ☐ *émeute* ☐ *congés*
4. shower (l. 17): ☐ *averse* ☐ *douche* ☐ *bain*

D. True or false? Justify in your own words.

1. T F Each family is allowed to spend a fixed number of carbon points per month.

....

2. T F Whenever (*à chaque fois que*) families buy food it costs them some carbon points.

....

3. T F When people buy a computer they lose points on their carbon card.

....

E. The expression "...fossil fuel" (l. 9) refers to:

☐ coal (*charbon*) ☐ sunlight ☐ water ☐ gas ☐ wind ☐ geothermal heat ☐ oil (*pétrole*)

F. Tick the correct statements.

1. Before last September, rich people lived as they wanted because:

☐ they could buy up extra carbon points. ☐ they did not care about the environment.

2. Since last September, rich people are allowed to use: ☐ 250 carbon points per month.

☐ 50 carbon points per month. ☐ all the carbon points they can buy.

G. What has become strictly forbidden?

☐ watching TV ☐ heating the house ☐ taking a shower ☐ having a fridge ☐ taking the plane

3 Part two

H. Observe the drawing on the carbon card and explain in your own words how people know that they have used up their carbon allowance.

....

....

4 Part three

I. Complete with words from the text.

1. As Laura's mother could not find her card, she asked Laura to .... her hers.
2. But the driver refused to let the mother on and said that if she did not have her own carbon ...., she could not have a ....
3. A woman was furious because she was waiting in the .... and Laura's mother was .... everybody.

Ten words to remember

Find the equivalents of these ten words (in the right order) and learn them by heart.

1. *allocation :*	6. *douche :* ....
2. *réellement /en fait :*	7. *bain :* ....
3. *chauffage :*	8. *sèche-cheveux :* ....
4. *carburant :*	9. *vol / voyage en avion :* ....
5. *émeute :*	10. *manquer / rater :* ....

ENRICHIR SON LEXIQUE – La pollution

Classez les mots du tableau dans la catégorie qui convient.

· pollute	· contaminate	· fumes	· depletion of the ozone layer
· environmentalist	· polluter	· smog	· oil slick
· protect	· endanger	· nuclear waste	· jeopardize
· global warming	· save	· pesticide	· ecologist
· respect	· exhaust	· fertilizer	
· preserve	· Green	· deforestation	

Someone who
protects the environment ....
destroys the environment ....

Action of (verbs)
protecting ....
destroying ....

Causes of pollution
....
....
....

PRATIQUER LA GRAMMAIRE

1 'S: IS ou HAS? → Précis grammatical 1, 2, 5, 43

A. Indiquez si 's correspond à IS ou HAS et identifiez la forme verbale soulignée en répondant aux questions suivantes :

a. présent (simple ou BE+ING) ou *present perfect?* – **b.** voix active ou passive?

Exemple : *...it's been shipped over from China...* (l. 8) : *has / present perfect /* voix passive

1. *...all the energy that's gone into making it.* (l. 10) ....
2. *...no one's allowed to buy...* (l. 13) ....
3. *She's been taken to the hospital.* ....
4. *He's made the wrong decision.* ....
5. *She's been given three choices.* ....
6. *He's giving her a lot of trouble.* ....

2 Indénombrables et articles → Précis grammatical 19

B. Complétez avec l'article A/AN, sinon inscrivez ø lorsque le nom est indénombrable.

1. *The room has* .... *heating,* .... *air-conditioning and* .... *private bathroom.*
2. *We had* .... *awful weather but it was* .... *wonderful trip.*
3. *I have* .... *important information for you.*
4. *Your Mum didn't give you* .... *very good advice, did she?*
5. *This is* .... *good news, isn't it?*
6. *He has* .... *opportunity to show he can do better.*

3 Emplois particuliers de l'article A/AN → Précis grammatical 21D

C. Justifiez chaque emploi de l'article A/AN à l'aide de l'une des propositions suivantes :

A/AN est utilisé : **a.** devant un nom de métier. **b.** après une préposition.
c. devant une expression de mesure ou de temps pour traduire « par ».

1. *...no one's allowed to buy more than 50 extra points a month.* (l. 13) ....
2. *It's all kind of a choice.* (l. 19) ....
3. *My father is a journalist.* ....

D. Complétez avec A/AN lorsque c'est nécessaire, sinon inscrivez ø.
(Attention : les noms indénombrables sont incompatibles avec l'article A/AN !)

1. *David will soon be out of* .... *work and without* .... *job, he might have to move.*
2. *My younger sister wants to be* .... *actress.*
3. *My brother visits our parents twice* .... *week.*
4. *We had* .... *nice flat with* .... *view of the Empire State Building.*
5. *He's been under* .... *great stress lately.*
6. *He was out in the cold without* .... *coat for over two hours.*

CHECK YOUR SKILLS

COMPRÉHENSION DE L'ORAL

Your CD 23 — CD 2/14

Comprendre une annonce à la radio

1. **Who made the announcement and how long was it broadcast?**
   The announcement was made by ...., it was broadcast (*diffusé*) from .... to ....
2. **Complete the sentences (one blank = one word)**
   a. Kimberly-Clark produces .... tissue paper products.
   b. The firm is blamed for not using .... paper for its products.
   c. As a consequence, ancient .... of North America are being destroyed.
3. **True or false? Justify with one or several keywords.**
   a. T F Most people think that Kleenex tissues are made from recycled paper. ....
   b. T F Kleenex tissue is made from trees which are a thousand years old. ....
4. **Where is the Boreal Forest located?** ....
5. **We should be concerned about this forest because of the threat of** ....
   .... **pollution.**
6. **What should we do? Complete (one blank = one word):**
   a. We should keep the trees in the .... and not in ....
   b. We should use tissue paper made with ....
7. **What is the 2009 agreement about?**
   - ☐ Taking measures to protect forests
   - ☐ Stopping making tissue paper products
   - ☐ Using wood from other forests
   - ☐ Using more and more recycled paper

Je me situe par rapport au CECRL

Questions	Quand j'écoute cette annonce à la radio, je peux :		☺	😐	☹
1	comprendre des informations précises simples.	A2			
2	comprendre le sujet général.	A2			
3-4-6	comprendre les points principaux d'une intervention.	B1			
5	comprendre les arguments utilisés par le locuteur.	B1			
7	comprendre le point de vue du locuteur.	B1			

EXPRESSION ORALE EN CONTINU

Parler d'un sujet de société

Je me situe par rapport au CECRL

Quand je parle de ce sujet de société, je peux :		☺	😐	☹
décrire la situation et le personnage avec des mots simples.	A2			
justifier très simplement mon opinion.	A2			
faire un exposé simple et développer les points importants avec précision.	B1			
expliquer mon opinion en donnant des arguments.	B1			
parler de manière compréhensible et sans trop hésiter, même si je fais des pauses pour réfléchir.	B1			

LISTENERS' CORNER
Is privacy dead?

LISTENING COMPREHENSION

CD 2 16-18

1 Get ready

A. Before listening to the interview, match the pronunciation of each word with its spelling:
a. soul (*âme*) – **b.** former (*précédent*) – **c.** reassure – **d.** social – **e.** available (*disponible*) – **f.** stored (*stocké*) – **g.** profile – **h.** research

1. /əˈveɪləbl/: ....
2. /ˈsəʊʃəl/: ....
3. /ˈfɔːmə/: ....
4. /rɪˈsɜːtʃ/: ....
5. /ˈprəʊfaɪl/: ....
6. /stɔːd/: ....
7. /səʊl/: ....
8. /ˌriːəˈʃʊə/: ....

2 Part one

B. List the four websites mentioned by the reporter. ....

....

C. What happens when people use these websites? ☐ They get private information from other users. ☐ They make their public information private. ☐ They make their private information public.

D. Complete this sentence: Steven Metcalf is an online ....

E. Number of pages of private information he got about the reporter: ☐ 5 ☐ 15 ☐ 16 ☐ 50

F. What private information did Steven Metcalf find about the reporter?

☐ His home address
☐ His phone number
☐ His wife's job
☐ His credit card number
☐ His social security number
☐ His former jobs
☐ His children's names
☐ The movies he likes
☐ The foods he likes

3 Part two

G. Complete these sentences. (one blank = one word)

1. Everytime people hit the *Send* button, personal information becomes ....
2. The products you buy or rent (*louer*) on the Internet can be ....
3. The searches you do on your Facebook profile can be viewed, ... and sometimes ....

H. "The Internet is a window into your soul." means that on the Internet people:
☐ know everything about you. ☐ don't know anything about you. ☐ make friends with you.

4 Part three

I. True or false? Justify orally.
T F All the information that you have posted on the net will stay on the net.

J. What did Google recently say? (one blank = one word)

a. It gives its web users the tools they need to .... their .... information.
b. People should be more ....about what they .... on the web.

K. According to Steven, nothing will be safer than people's own judgment and ....

TEXT 1

No need for Twitter

READING COMPREHENSION

A. Read the whole text and match paragraphs with titles:

Paragraph 1 •	• Adults' favourite hi-tech devices
Paragraph 2 •	• The popularity of Twitter among adults
Paragraph 3 •	• A teenager explains why she does not need Twitter
Paragraphs 4 and 5 •	• The reasons why young people do not use Twitter

B. Who has no need for Twitter according to the journalist? ....

C. Why does Kristen never use Twitter?

☐ She is too young.
☒ She thinks Twitter is strange.
☐ She is too old.
☒ She doesn't want anyone to know what she does.

D. True or false? Justify by quoting keywords.

1. T (F) Old people are not interested in video games. Nintendo wiis in nursing house
2. T (F) Hi-tech devices are not popular with adults. Iphone and GPS [...] adult only
3. (T) F Twitter's popularity comes from adults. ligne 18
4. (T) F Twitter is the first social website that has attracted adults. ligne 25

....

E. Tick the reasons which explain why young people aren't interested in Twitter.

☑ They already interact with friends via Facebook or text messaging.
☑ They want to interact with their friends only.
☑ Twitter is more for business purposes.
☐ They want to send longer messages.

PRATIQUER LA GRAMMAIRE

Les quantifieurs → Précis grammatical 22

F. Complétez avec *much*, *many*, *little* ou *few*.

1. *It seems that* .... *youngsters are using Facebook but very* .... *of them are interested in Twitter.*
2. *I've got very* .... *money and there are so* .... *things I'd like to buy!*
3. *How* .... *messages do you receive every day?*
4. *They haven't made* .... *progress, have they?*

G. Complétez avec *all*, *every* ou *whole*.

1. .... *student in the class was involved in the project.*
2. *Our project involved the* .... *school!*
3. *He's been waiting for this* .... *his life!*
4. *I like* .... *electronic gadgets!*

TEXT 2

Got a computer?

READING COMPREHENSION

1 Part one

A. Mr Rayment and his computer. True or false? Justify by quoting from the text.

1. T F Mr Rayment is addicted to his computer.

....

2. T F He does not surf the Internet.

....

3. T F Mr Rayment's computer is a state-of-the-art computer.

....

4. T F He thinks his computer cannot be connected to the net.

....

B. Try to define Drago's attitude.

1. Drago's "unbelieving smile" (l. 10) shows that he is:

☐ understanding ☐ puzzled (*perplexe*) ☐ angry ☐ happy

2. In your own words, explain his reaction:

....

3. Drago thinks Mr Rayment is: (Justify.)

☐ trendy (*branché*) ☐ understanding ☐ old-fashioned ☐ narrow-minded (*étroit d'esprit*)

....

C. Read the passage from l. 16 to l. 19. Quote the sentences indicating that:

1. Mr Rayment is trying to say exactly what he thinks.

....

2. He does not want Drago to make fun of him.

....

3. He thinks that time has gone by too quickly.

....

4. Mr Rayment's computer does not correspond to what Drago expected.

....

D. Tick the adjectives that best define Mr Rayment in this part.

☐ furious ☐ offended (*vexé*) ☐ understanding ☐ indifferent ☐ upset (*contrarié*)

2 Part two

E. Pick out one sentence showing that Drago doesn't understand Mr Rayment.

....

....

F. Tick the correct translation of

1. once upon a time (l. 21):

☐ *il était une fois* ☐ *autrefois* ☐ *il n'y a pas si longtemps* ☐ *un jour ou l'autre*

2. time got to work on me (l. 23):

☐ *Le temps ne se rattrape jamais.* ☐ *Le temps a fini par m'user.* ☐ *Le temps n'a eu aucun effet sur moi.*

G. According to Mr Rayment why do people become old-fashioned? Quote two sentences.

....

....

H. Why does Drago tell Mr Rayment about his grandparents? To show that (several anwers):

☐ even old people can adapt to modern life. ☐ his mother is generous.

☐ Mr Rayment could react differently. ☐ anyone can surf the net.

I. Does Mr Rayment understand why Drago talks about his grandparents?

☐ yes ☐ no Justify with a one-word sentence: ....

Ten words to remember

Find the equivalents of these words in the text (in the right order) and learn them by heart.

1. *cordon :* ....

2. *relier :* ....

3. *sorte de :* ....

4. *moderne :* ....

5. *haïr :* ....

6. *se moquer de :* ....

7. *être à la hauteur :* ....

8. *regarder fixement :* ....

9. *perplexité :* ....

10. *démodé :* ....

ENRICHIR SON LEXIQUE – L'informatique

Across

2. To copy CDs or DVDs

3. A device used to type text or numbers

6. The worldwide web

7. A device that links computers through a telephone line

8. The address of a web page

10. A computer programme

12. A disk that is used to store data (*données*)

Down

1. The international network

4. To copy or transfer data from computer to computer

5. A hand-held device used to click on the screen

9. A computer screen

11. An Internet connection without cables

PRATIQUER LA GRAMMAIRE

1 Présent simple et présent *BE+ING* → Précis grammatical 1, 2, 3

A. Formez un énoncé au présent simple ou au présent *BE+ING*.

1. *(he – often – use) his computer?*

....

2. *Can you repeat please? (I – not – understand) what (you – talk about).*

....

3. *(you – think) I (not – know) what (you – do) here?*

....

4. *(you – tell) me that (I – need) to buy a new one?*

....

2 *HAVE* et *HAVE GOT*

B. Lisez ces énoncés puis indiquez pour chacun d'eux si *HAVE* est utilisé en tant que verbe ou en tant qu'auxiliaire.

1. *Do you* ***have*** *a cord somewhere that links you into the net?* (l. 7) ....
2. *I'****ve*** *got a computer.* ....
3. *He doesn't* ***have*** *much to say.* ....

C. Mettez les énoncés ci-dessous à la forme interrogative.

1. *He's got a new mobile.* ....
2. *She has an interesting job.* ....
3. *You have something to say.* ....

D. Donnez deux traductions des énoncés suivants, l'une avec le verbe *HAVE*, l'autre avec *HAVE GOT*.

1. Est-ce qu'il a un iPhone ? ....

....

2. Il n'a pas beaucoup de temps. ....

....

3 *THIS, THAT, THESE, THOSE* → Précis grammatical 24

E. Qu'expriment *THIS, THAT, THESE* et *THOSE* dans chacun des énoncés ci-dessous :

1. la proximité **2.** l'éloignement ? Cochez la case correspondante dans le tableau ci-dessous.

F. Traduisez le passage en gras dans la colonne correspondante.

	1	2	Traduction
1. *"No, it's not* ***that kind of computer****."* (l. 8)	☐	☐	....
2. *"****This was all****, once upon a time, new."* (l. 21)	☐	☐	....
3. ***This is*** *my uncle, George Watkins.*	☐	☐	....
4. ***These days*** *computers are everywhere.*	☐	☐	....
5. *Nobody had a computer* ***in those days****.*	☐	☐	....

CHECK YOUR SKILLS

COMPRÉHENSION DE L'ÉCRIT

Comprendre un extrait de presse

1. **Tick the correct answers. The article is about:**
   □ making pirate DVDs in China. □ exploiting Chinese workers in the UK.
   □ illegal export of pirate DVDs to the UK. □ DVD piracy in the UK.
2. **Quote two elements illustrating each of the following ideas.**
   a. The difficult conditions of Chinese workers.
   ....
   b. DVD piracy is a profitable business.
   ....
3. **True or false? Circle the correct answer and justify by quoting keywords.**
   a. T F The piracy business started small and developed rapidly. ....
   ....
   b. T F The pirates were found guilty. ....
   c. T F The police arrested the criminals by chance. ....
4. **What is the main idea in the last sentence?**
   □ Chinese workers are invisible. □ The trip to the UK cost them £ 20,000. □ They work like slaves.
5. **According to the journalist, who are the main victims of the piracy? Quote from the text.**
   ....

Je me situe par rapport au CECRL

Questions	Quand je lis cet article, je peux :		☺	😐	☹
1	identifier l'information principale.	A2			
2	y trouver des informations précises.	A2			
3	en reconnaître les points significatifs.	B1			
4	distinguer l'idée essentielle des détails.	B1			
5	identifier la principale conclusion de l'argumentation.	B1			

EXPRESSION ÉCRITE

Écrire sur un sujet familier

Je me situe par rapport au CECRL

Quand j'écris sur ce sujet familier, je peux :		☺	😐	☹
faire une description élémentaire dans une langue simple.	A2			
écrire à propos de mon environnement quotidien.	A2			
relier les différentes parties de mon texte par des mots simples tels que *and*, *but*, *because*.	A2			
exposer mes goûts particuliers sans utiliser trop souvent le dictionnaire.	B1			
exprimer un point de vue personnel.	B1			
structurer mon texte en utilisant des mots de liaison variés.	B1			
supprimer en me relisant les erreurs de langue les plus importantes.	B1			

LISTENERS' CORNER
Horror films

LISTENING COMPREHENSION

CD 2 / 28-30

1 Get ready

A. Before listening to the interview, make sure that you recognize the following words. The translations of three words are given. Find out the others.

1. /friːk/ freak: *monstre*
2. /'ʃɪvə/ shiver: *frisson*
3. /ðə kriːps/ the creeps: *la chair de poule*
4. /friːkɪ/ freaky: ....
5. /θrɪl/ thrill: ....
6. /'skɛərɪ/ scary: ....
7. /fɪə/ fear: ....
8. /'naɪtmɛə/ nightmare: ....
9. /'gɔːrɪ/ gory: ....
10. /'saɪkəʊpæθ/ psychopath: ....

2 General comprehension

B. What is the name of the radio programme? ....

C. What horror film(s) does each interviewee mention? Indicate for each film if he / she liked (+) or didn't like (–) it.

1. Dorothy: ....
2. Tom: ....
3. Sarah: ....

3 Part one

D. Listen to Dorothy twice and tick all the words she uses to talk about horror films.

☐ the creeps ☐ terrifying ☐ stunning ☐ scared ☐ thrills ☐ impressed
☐ scariest ☐ freaky ☐ fear ☐ crazy ☐ oppressive ☐ nightmares

4 Part two

E. True or false? Circle the correct answer and justify.

1. T F Tom doesn't like watching scary movies alone.

....

2. T F The main character in Tom's favourite movie is quite funny.

....

5 Part three

F. What are the characteristics of a psychological thriller? (one blank = one word)

SARAH: Take .... for example: there's no ...., there's no ...., no .... or ...., and it's still really ....

G. Why doesn't Sarah like the second film she mentions?

SARAH: I thought that that was one of the most .... films ever made. (...) The atmosphere is so .... and the characters are so ...., it just made me really .... I really found it .... !

TEXT 1

The giant

READING COMPREHENSION

A. True or False? Justify by quoting from the text.

1. T F The action takes place when the narrator's father was a young man.

....

2. T F Facing the giant was dangerous.

....

B. Find the English translation of the word *ramper*: ....

C. What sort of food was the giant interested in?

1. .... 2. ....

D. Quote a sentence indicating that the villagers did not know how to react to the giant's pillaging.

....

E. Deduce the meaning of the sentence of "father set out on his way" (l. 16)

Mon père ☐ *se perdit en chemin.* ☐ *se mit en chemin.* ☐ *demanda son chemin.*

F. Find the English translation of the word *grotte*: ....

G. What shows that the giant does not take the father seriously? Quote at least one sentence.

....

H. Use your answer to find the English tanslation of the noun *sourire*: ....

I. What word made him change his mind? ....

J. The giant realizes that the father accepts to be ....

PRATIQUER LA GRAMMAIRE

Le génitif → Précis grammatical 20

G. Formez un génitif à partir des éléments en gras.

1. ***The power of Karl*** *seemed unlimited.*

....

2. ***The field belonging to Chris*** *had been ravaged.*

....

3. ***The decision made by our neighbours*** *was quite unexpected.*

....

4. *He had never heard the sound of* ***the voice of the Giant****.*

....

5. ***The house owned by my parents*** *was located in Ashland.*

....

TEXT 2
The man who could see

READING COMPREHENSION

1 Part one

A. Use the context to guess the meaning of the following words:

1. brain (l. 3) : ☐ *mémoire* ☐ *cerveau* ☐ *esprit*
2. diseased (l. 6) : ☐ *malade* ☐ *larmoyant* ☐ *sain*
3. eyelashes (l. 7) : ☐ *joues* ☐ *cils* ☐ *narines*
4. eyelids (l. 8 - lid = *couvercle*) : ☐ *sourcils* ☐ *paupières* ☐ *orbites*
5. remove (l. 13) : ☐ *bouger* ☐ *retirer* ☐ *ouvrir*

B. Complete the sentence.

According to the doctor, Nunez's brain is affected because his .... are ....

C. True or false? Justify by quoting from the text.

1. T F The eyes of the blind only play an aesthetic role.

....

2. T F Nunez's eyes are similar to the eyes of blind people.

....

3. T F According to the doctor, Nunez's brain is constantly irritated because of his eyes.

....

4. T F The doctor proposes a radical solution.

....

5. T F The doctor does not think that Nunez will be cured.

....

D. Explain in your own words what "being sane" means for the blind.

....

E. What verb indicates that Yacob did not expect Nunez to react in such a way?

....

F. Why is Yacob disappointed? Because (several answers):

☐ Nunez strikes him.
☐ Nunez may not really love his daughter.
☐ he expected Nunez to be enthusiastic.
☐ Nunez refuses to have an operation.

2 Part two

G. The sentence: "It was Medina-sarote ... the blind surgeons" (l. 22) indicates that:

☐ she managed to convince him to undergo (*subir*) the operation to lose his sight.
☐ she did not succeed in convincing him to be operated on.

H. Find the nouns corresponding to the following definitions:

1. a natural aptitude or ability: ....
2. the faculty of seeing: ....
3. destiny: ....

I. How does Nunez react at first? (several answers)

☐ He hesitates to accept the doctors' proposal.
☐ He accepts the proposal.
☐ He explains to Medina-sarote what losing sight means for him.
☐ He tells her that he won't be able to see her anymore.

J. What shows that Medina-sarote does not understand what seeing is? Quote:

....

K. The word "sympathy" (l. 33) is a false friend. It means:

☐ *amitié* ☐ *compassion* ☐ *amour* ☐ *colère* ☐ *dégoût*

L. Use the context to deduce the meaning of "lack" (l. 33) then explain why Nunez feels sympathy for Medina-sarote:

....

M. Complete the girl's sentence: "If only you would ....

....

Ten words to remember

Find the equivalents of these ten words in the text (in the right order) and learn them by heart.

1. *cerveau :* ....
2. *cil :* ....
3. *paupière :* ....
4. *guérir :* ....
5. *citoyen :* ....
6. *vue :* ....
7. *coucher de soleil :* ....
8. *doux / douce :* ....
9. *destin :* ....
10. *manque :* ....

ENRICHIR SON LEXIQUE – La vue

Les expressions suivantes contiennent le mot *eye* ou font allusion à la vue. Traduisez-les, à l'aide d'un dictionnaire si nécessaire.

1. *have an eye-test* ....
2. *be short-sighted* ....
3. *be far/long-sighted* ....
4. *be colour-blind* ....
5. *to my eyes* ....
6. *eyes wide open* ....
7. *keep an eye on somebody* ....
8. *make eye contact* ....
9. *invisible to the naked eye* ....
10. *make eyes at somebody* ....
11. *have eyes like a hawk* ....
12. *for your eyes only* ....
13. *have eyes bigger than your belly* ....
14. *An eye for an eye* ....
15. *In the country of the blind the one-eyed man is king.* ....

....

PRATIQUER LA GRAMMAIRE

1 Proposition infinitive → Précis grammatical 33

A. Observez les propositions infinitives soulignées dans les énoncés suivants :

1. *... her father, Yacob, wants Nunez to be examined by a blind doctor.* (l. 2)
2. *"You do not want me," he said, "to lose my gift of sight?"* (l. 23)
3. *She told him to go and see her father.*

Quelle est la forme du pronom dans la proposition infinitive? ☐ sujet ☐ complément

B. Formez des énoncés avec les éléments donnés. Faites les modifications nécessaires.

1. *He told (I – look after – you).* ....
2. *I'll ask (they – leave – you alone).* ....
3. *Do you really want (we – stay)?* ....
4. *Did you really ask (she – accept that deal)?* ....

2 Les relatifs *WHO* et *THAT* → Précis grammatical 38

C. Indiquez pour chaque énoncé :

a. quel est l'antécédent du pronom relatif. **b.** si le pronom est sujet ou complément de la relative.

Les parenthèses signifient que le pronom *THAT* peut être effacé.

1. *The man* ***who*** *could see.* ....
2. *Those queer things* ***that*** *are called the eyes* [...] (l. 5) ....
3. *Here is the doctor* ***(that)*** *I've told you about.* ....
4. *The place* ***(that)*** *I have visited is very strange.* ....

D. Complétez avec *WHO* ou *THAT* (*THAT* peut être effacé).

1. *This is the message* .... *he sent me.*
2. *The girl* .... *is talking to you is my sister.*
3. *The people* .... *sent him there were crazy.*
4. *The only person* .... *we spoke to was a doctor.*

3 *WOULD*

E. Dans quel(s) énoncés *WOULD* exprime-t-il une nuance de volonté : 1. ☐ 2. ☐ ou 3. ☐ ?

1. *"I wish sometimes... you would not talk like that."* (l. 29)
2. *"Oh, if you would," she sobbed, "if only you would!"* (l. 37)
3. *If I accepted that, I would lose my sight.*

F. Traduisez les énoncés ci-dessus.

1. ....

....

2. ....

....

3. ....

....

CHECK YOUR SKILLS

COMPRÉHENSION DE L'ÉCRIT

Comprendre un extrait de roman

1. What has Dorian decided to do?

....

2. Why? Quote: ....

3. Where do the two main scenes take place?

a. .... b. ....

4. True or false. Justify with keywords.

a. [T] [F] Sybil expected (*s'attendait à*) Dorian's decision. ....

b. [T] [F] She tried to dissuade him. ....

c. [T] [F] She cried when she realized there was nothing she could do. ....

5. What are Dorian's feelings for Sybil?

☐ love ☐ pity ☐ contempt (*mépris*) ☐ irritation ☐ tenderness

6. Why was Dorian surprised when he saw his portrait? Quote:

....

7. Compare (quote):

His face on the portrait	....
His face in the mirror	....

Je me situe par rapport au CECRL

Questions	Quand je lis cet extrait de roman, je peux :		☺	😐	☹
1-3	trouver une information particulière.	A2			
2-6	identifier l'information principale.	A2			
4-7	comprendre l'essentiel de la narration.	B1			
5	comprendre les descriptions de sentiments.	B1			

EXPRESSION ORALE EN CONTINU

Parler d'un film

Je me situe par rapport au CECRL

Quand je parle de ce film, je peux :		☺	😐	☹
décrire les personnages avec des mots simples.	A2			
en raconter l'histoire en quelques phrases simples.	A2			
en raconter l'intrigue, dire si je l'ai aimé ou non, et expliquer pourquoi.	B1			
parler de manière compréhensible même si je fais des pauses pour réfléchir.	B1			

LISTENERS' CORNER
The Canadian mosaic

LISTENING COMPREHENSION

CD 2 41-42

1 Get ready

A. Before listening to the recording, match each word with its definition. Write the corresponding letter in each blank.

1. Caucasian /kɔːˈkeɪzɪən/: ....
2. fowl /faʊl/: ....
3. hybrid /ˈhaɪbrɪd/: ....
4. evolve /ɪˈvɒlv/: ....
5. eventually /ɪˈventʃʊəlɪ/: ....
6. fortunate /ˈfɔːtʃənɪt/: ....

a. finally – **b.** lucky – **c.** a bird that is kept for its meat or eggs – **d.** a member of the race of people with white or pale skin – **e.** develop and change – **f.** a person whose parents are of different ethnical origins.

2 Part one

B. Listen to Kit Wong twice and complete this passage while and after listening. (one blank = one word)

Kit Wong educated his children, a .... and a ...., in the same traditional .... way his parents .... him. But if they marry a ...., he believes that they will lose their .... and their .... The problem is that they speak more .... than ....

C. Does Terry Woo ☐ agree or ☐ disagree with Kit Wong? Justify by quoting him.

1. ....
2. ....
3. ....
4. ....

3 Part two

D. Listen to Judy once and complete the following portrait.

1. She is ☐ Chinese ☐ Caucasian. Her husband is ☐ Chinese ☐ Caucasian.
2. Where did she grow up? ....
3. When she says that she feels "neither fish nor fowl", she means that she feels neither .... nor ....
4. When she says that she had her "nose pressed against the window looking in", she means that she was: ☐ too curious ☐ very curious ☐ not curious at all.
5. What is her profession? ....
6. What word does she use to define herself, her children and Terry Woo? ....

E. Listen to Judy a second time and complete this passage. (one blank = one word)

According to Judy, Canada is a country of ...., because it accepts so many different .... and it allows these cultures to .... These different cultures will eventually .... something truly ....

F. How does Judy feel about living in Canada? Quote two adjectives: ....

Unit 6
page 96

TEXT 1

Sharing a flat

READING COMPREHENSION

A. Find the equivalents of the following words (in the order of the text).

1. *logement* : ....
2. *candidat* : ....
3. *loyer* : ....
4. *sous-sol* : ....

B. Fill in the blanks (one blank = one word)

Sandy is looking for a .... which she wants to .... ; so she .... Wilma who lives in .... and .... her to tea.

C. Answer the questions.

1. Why did Sandy choose to phone Wilma? ....
....
2. Why did Sandy say "...we might be cousins?" (l. 23) ....
3. Why are they most probably not? ....

D. True or false? Circle the correct answer and justify your answer.

1. T F The rent was not very expensive.
....
2. T F The house was very quiet.
....
3. T F Sandy hesitated a long time before she decided to share the flat.
....

E. Write down the sentence corresponding to: (...) *néanmoins il n'y avait là rien qu'une couche de peinture et qu'une nouvelle porte d'entrée n'auraient pu arranger.*

....

PRATIQUER LA GRAMMAIRE

SOME, ANY, NO → Précis grammatical 22

Complétez avec *SOME*, *ANY* ou *NO*.

1. *Have .... more coffee.*
2. *I haven't seen you for .... time.*
3. *There aren't .... other people living in this flat.*
4. *I simply don't need .... help, thank you!*
5. *Why didn't .... other students turn up?*
6. *It was freezing and she had .... coat on.*
7. *Do you have .... idea where my cousin has gone?*
8. *Can I have .... more details, please?*
9. *I really see .... reason why you shouldn't rent that flat.*
10. *Make yourself comfortable. There's .... place like home!*

TEXT 2
Dhowli

READING COMPREHENSION

1 Part one

A. Use the context to match the words and expressions with the translation.

a. *larme* – b. *douleur* – c. *se débarrasser de* – d. *désespéré*

1. tear (l. 6) ....
3. pain (l. 7) ....
2. hopeless (l. 7) ....
4. get rid of (l. 14) ....

B. True or false? Circle the correct answer and justify by quoting from the text.

1. T F There is no electricity in Dhowli's house.
....
2. T F Dhowli and her mother share a bed.
....
3. T F Dhowli's mother did not understand why her daughter was crying.
....
4. T F Dhowli's mother thought they would have to leave the village.
....
5. T F Dhowli's mother is only worried about herself.
....
6. T F Dhowli is pregnant.
....

2 Part two

C. Use the context to match the words and expressions with the translation.

a. *parents* – b. *mettre à la porte* – c. *embêter* – d. *élever* – e. *voler* – f. *prendre soin de*

1. bring up (l. 16) ....
4. steal (l. 32) ....
2. look after (l. 19) ....
5. annoy (l. 34) ....
3. folks (l. 29) ....
6. throw out (l. 35) ....

D. Complete the sentences. Use as many words from the text as you can.

1. Dhowli's mother thinks the Misras should ....
....
2. Dhowli refuses to say anything to the Misras, because she ....
....
3. The Misras' son promised Dhowli that ....
4. Dhowli believes that the Misras' son is not like the others because ....
5. According to Dhowli, the Misras' son has not visited his parents these past months because ....
....

E. Answer the questions.

1. Why does Dhowli's mother think she is the victim of injustice? ....

....

2. Why is Dhowli's mother ready to do? ....

Ten words to remember

Find the equivalents of these words in the text (in the right order) and learn them by heart.

1. *souffler :* ....
2. *larme :* ....
3. *pleurer :* ....
4. *se débarrasser de :* ....
5. *élever :* ....
6. *prendre soin de :* ....
7. *se tenir à l'écart :* ....
8. *voler :* ....
9. *punir :* ....
10. *fâché :* ....

ENRICHIR SON LEXIQUE – Les verbes à particule

→ Précis grammatical 18

A. Traduisez les verbes à particules soulignés dans les phrases ci-dessous extraites du texte.

1. *Her mother saw her come in...* (l. 3) ....
2. *Dhowli blew out the lamp...* (l. 5) ....
3. *She lay down beside her mother.* (l. 6) ....
4. *"The Misras should help to bring up the child."* (l. 16) ....
5. *"It would have been different if he came back."* (l. 17) ....
6. *"Is that why he has stayed away in Dhanbad..."* (l. 28) ....
7. *"Throw me out, then."* (l. 35) ....

B. Complétez les phrases avec la particule qui convient. Chaque particule ne peut-être employée qu'une fois.

across – away – back – down – in – off – on – out – through – up

1. *Keep* .... *! Don't stop now.*
2. *Because of the wind they could not put the fire* ....
3. *As soon as he arrives, show him* ....
4. *This case is too heavy, I'll put it* .... *for a minute.*
5. *Make* .... *your mind! I can't wait for hours.*
6. *Be polite, don't answer* ....
7. *It is sunny, so the snow has melted* ....
8. *Turn* .... *the light, please.*
9. *She anxiously read the letter* ....
10. *Lindbergh flew* .... *the Atlantic in 1927.*

PRATIQUER LA GRAMMAIRE

1 Subordonnées en *IF* → Précis grammatical 9B

A. Lisez les passages ci-dessous et répondez aux questions a et b.

1. *It would have been different if he had come back.*
2. *It would be different if he came back.*
3. *If he comes back, we will tell him what to do.*

a. Associez à chacune des explications suivantes la subordonnée en *IF* qui lui correspond :
– C'est une hypothèse qui se réalisera peut-être dans l'avenir : ....
– C'est une hypothèse incertaine (mais qui pourrait se réaliser) : ....
– C'est une hypothèse qui ne s'est pas réalisée : ....

b. Traduisez les énoncés 1, 2 et 3.

1. ....
2. ....
3. ....

B. Mettez le verbe entre parenthèses à la forme qui convient au présent, au prétérit ou au *pluperfect*.

1. *Would he look after you if you (ask) .... him to?*
2. *If she really (love) .... him, she'll wait for him.*
3. *If you (not – be) .... so selfish, you would understand me.*
4. *If I (know) ...., I would have thrown you out.*
5. *If you (not – change) .... your mind right now, you'll have to leave.*
6. *They would kill you if you (try) .... to run away.*

2 *They, them, their, theirs, they're, there's* → Précis grammatical 23

C. Complétez avec l'un des éléments donnés ci-dessus.

1. .... *think that* .... *something wrong with* .... *daughter.*
2. *It's not our fault, it's* ....*!*
3. .... *not doing anything to help* .... *own folk!*
4. *Tell* .... *that* .... *nothing we can do about it.*

3 *To* dans les énoncés de reprise → Précis grammatical 30, 33A

D. Retrouvez dans le texte les passages correspondant à ces deux énoncés et écrivez entre parenthèses les mots qui sont sous-entendus.

1. "*If I have to.*" (l. 12) (........................)
2. "*He promised to.*" (l. 20) (........................)

E. Traduisez les énoncés 1 et 2 en français.

1. ....
2. ....

CHECK YOUR SKILLS

COMPRÉHENSION DE L'ORAL

Comprendre un reportage

• **Sophia Wang**

Avant d'écoutez le document sonore lisez les mots ci-dessous.

Korean /kə'rɪən/: *coréen* – Jewish /'dʒu:ɪʃ/: *juif* – bother /'bɒðə/ : *déranger*

1. **Age ?** ……………… **Where does she live ?** ………………
2. **Write down the adjectives Sophia uses to mention her parents origins:**
   a. her mother : ……………… ……………… ………………
   b. her father : ……………… ………………
3. **Sophia says she is a ☐ half-race ☐ mixed-race ☐ multi-race ☐ many-race person.**
4. **When she is at the Hebrew (*hébraïque*) school, why does Sophia feel different? Is that a problem for her?**
   ………………………………
5. **Why does Sophia feel comfortable everywhere she goes? Write down what she says.**
   ………………………………

• **Hannah Motley**

6. **Age?** ……………… **Origins?** ………………
7. **Black people consider she is** ……………… **; white people consider she is** ………………
8. **What does she say she is?** ………………
9. **What happens sometimes when her mother picks her up from school?**
   ………………………………

Je me situe par rapport au CECRL

Questions	Quand j'écoute ce reportage, je peux :		☺	😐	☹
1-6-7	en comprendre le sujet général ainsi que des informations simples.	A2			
2-3-8	en comprendre les points principaux ainsi que des points de détail.	B1			
4-5-9	reconnaître le point de vue des locuteurs.	B1			

EXPRESSION ORALE EN CONTINU

Parler d'un sujet de societé

Je me situe par rapport au CECRL

Quand je parle de ce sujet de société, je peux :		☺	😐	☹
décrire la situation et les personnages avec des mots simples.	A2			
justifier très simplement mon opinion.	A2			
faire un exposé simple et développer les points importants avec précision.	B1			
expliquer mon opinion en donnant des arguments.	B1			
parler de manière compréhensible et sans trop hésiter, même si je fais des pauses pour réfléchir.	B1			

LISTENERS' CORNER
London today

LISTENING COMPREHENSION

CD 3/ 2-4

1 Get ready

A. Before listening to the recording, match the pronunciation of each word with its spelling.

a. filthy (*dégoûtant*) – **b.** unaffordable (*hors de prix*) – **c.** survival – **d.** bustling (*plein de vie*) – **e.** tattoo – **f.** pierce – **g.** siren

1. /'saɪərən/ : .... **2.** /'bʌslɪŋ/ : .... **3.** /sə'vaɪvəl/ : .... **4.** /ʌnə'fɔːdəbl/ : ....

5. /pɪəs/ : .... **6.** /tə'tuː/ : .... **7.** /'fɪlθɪ/ : ....

2 Part one

B. Tick the five adjectives Pamela uses to qualify London (in the right order).

☐ noisy ☐ busy ☐ dirty ☐ filthy ☐ expensive ☐ polluted ☐ lively (*animé*)
☐ unaffordable ☐ crowded ☐ comfortable ☐ dangerous ☐ populous ☐ unsafe

C. According to Pamela, what makes London so noisy? Write keywords.

1. .... 3. ....
2. .... 4. ....

D. What prevents people from walking on pavements? (two answers)

☐ overflowing litter bins (*poubelles qui débordent*) ☐ dog mess (*crottes*) ☐ plastic bottles and cups

☐ sleeping bums (*clochards*) ☐ skateboarders ☐ torn waste bags (*sacs poubelles déchirés*)

3 Part two

E. Complete this passage with Pamela's words. (one blank = one word)

Pamela can't have .... or normal .... because London is a combat .... where you must always be in .... mode.

F. Why doesn't Pamela move? ....

4 Part three

G. Patrick agrees with Pamela about the following problems:

1. .... 2. ....

H. Which words show that London is:

1. a cosmopolitan city? ....
2. a city where you can be yourself? ....

I. Where did Patrick take his kids last Saturday?

1. .... 3. ....
2. .... 4. ....

TEXT 1
The Big Brother reality

READING COMPREHENSION

A. Find the equivalents of the following words (in the order of the text)

1. *moyenne :* ....
2. *près de :* ....
3. *cauchemar :* ....
4. *ombre :* ....

B. When was *1984* written ? ....

C. Find one adjective which qualifies George Orwell: ....

D. Find one expression which describes his novel *1984*: ....

E. What details show the importance of video surveillance around George Orwell's house? Write down keywords.

....

....

F. What figures (*chiffres*) indicate that Orwell's house is not the only place to be watched in Great Britain?

....

G. What is the main idea of the article? Complete:

What Orwell imagined in *1948* has become ....

....

PRATIQUER LA GRAMMAIRE

Les participes passés irréguliers → Verbes irréguliers p. 206-207

H. Mettez les verbes entre parenthèses à la forme qui convient.

1. *The photograh was (choose)* .... *by me.*
2. *The jogger was (beat)* .... *to death by two youngsters.*
3. *She was (drive)* .... *home by a police officer.*
4. *It will be (do)* .... *within the next few days.*
5. *The paintings were (steal)* .... *last night.*
6. *Why is it (forbid)* .... *to take photographs in this area?*
7. *The police had (take)* .... *his passport away.*
8. *Careful! The chair is (break)* ....
9. *The camera was (hide)* .... *behind the curtains.*
10. *I'm afraid the document has been (throw)* .... *away.*

TEXT 2
Moving

READING COMPREHENSION

1 General comprehension

A. Complete the following summary.

Before moving, the narrator lived in .... , a district of ....
When she was .... years old her family moved to .... , a remote (*éloigné*) suburb. She stayed there for .... years, until she was .... , when she .... for good.

2 Part one

B. Tick the correct translation of each of the following words.

1. casually (l. 1): □ *d'un air gêné* □ *en passant* □ *d'un air sentencieux* □ *en insistant*
2. chitchat (l. 6): □ *quartier* □ *sentiment* □ *bavardage* □ *raison*
3. uproot (l. 8): □ *déraciner* □ *enraciner* □ *réveiller* □ *enfermer*
4. attend (l. 11): □ *attendre* □ *écouter* □ *aller à* □ *être au service de*

C. In the 4th paragraph, find the words corresponding to these definitions (in the right order).

1. to move about without any definite goal or destination: ....
2. feeling of anger: ....
3. free from danger: ....
4. to refuse: ....
5. to look fixedly: ....

D. In the 4th paragraph, find the English equivalents of these words (not in the right order).

1. *quartier :* ....
2. *traîner :* ....
3. *faire le trajet banlieue-ville :* ....

E. Read from l. 9 to l. 22 again and list the advantages of Fulham. Write keywords.

1. ....
2. ....
3. ....
4. ....
5. ....
6. ....
7. ....
8. ....
9. ....
10. ....
11. ....
12. ....
13. ....
14. ....

3 Part two

F. Find the words or expressions corresponding to these definitions (in the right order).

1. a large number of houses that have been built together in a planned way: ....
2. extremely large in size: ....
3. suburbs in general, and the behaviour, opinions and ways of living that are typical of people who live there – often used to show disapproval: ....
4. to accept a situation you do not like because you cannot change it: ....

5. a school for advanced education, especially in a particular profession: ....
6. to tremble because you are cold or frightened: ....
7. to be regarded or treated with disapproval: ....

G. In "featureless" (l. 24), the suffix *-less* shows that something is missing. What is missing?

☐ people ☐ characteristics ☐ friends ☐ life ☐ money ☐ time

H. True or false? Circle the correct answer and justify by quoting from the text.

1. T F Most people who lived on the housing estates were unemployed. ....
....
2. T F The narrator did not leave her grammar school in Fulham. ....
....
3. T F The narrator's father did not mind when she was late. ....
....

Ten words to remember

Find the equivalents of these ten words in the text (in the right order) and learn them by heart.

1. *déménager :* ....
2. *déraciner :* ....
3. *faire partie de :* ....
4. *proche :* ....
5. *faire le trajet banlieue-ville :* ....
6. *traîner :* ....
7. *voisinage, quartier :* ....
8. *campagne :* ....
9. *lotissement :* ....
10. *habitant :* ....

ENRICHIR SON LEXIQUE – La ville

Traduisez les mots du tableau. Aidez-vous d'un dictionnaire si nécessaire.

Noms				Verbes	
town hall	....	*phone booth*	....	*gather*	....
district	....	*taxi rank*	....	*lose contact*	....
skyscraper	....	*rush hour*	....	*be anonymous*	....
council flat	....	*traffic jam*	....	*rush*	....
block of flats	....	*traffic lights*	....	*queue up*	....
outer suburbs	....	*crossroads*	....	*call a cab*	....
dormitory town	....	*bus lane*	....	*settle*	....
green belt	....	*car park*	....	*mug*	....
slum area	....	*passer-by*	....	*stroll*	....
housing problems	....	*pedestrian crossing*	....	*go window-shopping*	....
pavement (GB) sidewalk (US)	....	*tube (GB) subway (US)*	....	*collect rubbish*	....

PRATIQUER LA GRAMMAIRE

1 Le gérondif → Précis grammatical 34

A. a. Lisez les énoncés suivants et indiquez à la suite de chacun si la forme en gras est un infinitif ou un gérondif en cochant la case correspondante.

1. *I spent the next days* ***wandering*** *around...* (l. 14) ☐ infinitif ☐ gérondif
2. *... I was plunged into* ***commuting****...* (l. 18) ☐ infinitif ☐ gérondif
3. *... all the inhabitants worked [...]* ***to pay*** *their mortgages.* (l. 26) ☐ infinitif ☐ gérondif
4. *I just want* ***to go*** *home.* ☐ infinitif ☐ gérondif

b. Les formes au gérondif ci-dessus expriment-elles **1.** un but à atteindre ou **2.** une activité ? ....

c. Répondez à la même question pour les formes à l'infinitif : ....

B. Mettez le verbe entre parenthèses à l'infinitif ou au gérondif.

1. *She couldn't put up with (live)* .... *in Perivale.*
2. *I left home (gain)* .... *more independence.*
3. *They were busy (work)* ....
4. *I'll spend the weekend (study)* ....

2 Le *pluperfect* → Précis grammatical 8

C. a. Lisez les énoncés suivants et indiquez à la suite de chacun si le verbe en gras est un prétérit ou un *pluperfect* en cochant la case correspondante.

1. *... my father casually* ***announced*** *to my sister and me...* (l. 1) ☐ prétérit ☐ *pluperfect*
2. *... [my father]* ***had*** *just* ***issued*** *the children...* (l. 5) ☐ prétérit ☐ *pluperfect*
3. *... I* ***walked out*** *with no money...* (l. 33) ☐ prétérit ☐ *pluperfect*
4. *I* ***had left*** *suburbia...* (l. 34) ☐ prétérit ☐ *pluperfect*

b. Quel(s) verbe(s) introduit (introduisent) un événement nouveau qui fait avancer le récit ?

....

c. Quel(s) verbe(s) permet (permettent) de commenter les événements en faisant un retour en arrière ?

....

D. Complétez les phrases interrogatives suivantes.

1. *He announced the news. → What* .... *he* ....?
2. *She had worked in the library. → Where* .... *she* ....?
3. *She had attended the youth club. → Which club* .... *she* ....?

3 Les prépositions *TO* et *FOR* → Précis grammatical 34

E. Quelle est la valeur de *TO* et *FOR* dans les passages suivants ? Cochez la bonne case.

1. *"To Perivale."* (l. 2) : déplacement ☐ dans l'espace ☐ dans le temps
2. *To this day...* (l. 8) : déplacement ☐ dans l'espace ☐ dans le temps
3. *... my 15-minute walk to school...* (l. 16) : déplacement ☐ dans l'espace ☐ dans le temps
4. *... for hours on end...* (l. 18): ☐ durée ☐ cause
5. *For the next six years...* (l. 28) ☐ durée ☐ cause
6. *... for coming home...* (l. 32) ☐ durée ☐ cause

CHECK YOUR SKILLS

COMPRÉHENSION DE L'ORAL

Your CD 40-41 — CD 3/ 13-14

Comprendre un interview

1. How old is Sarah? .... How old is Joan? ....
2. What question do they answer?

....

3. What do they think about the project? (one word)

Sarah: .... Joan: ....

4. Write down two of their arguments.

Sarah : 1. .... 2. ....

Joan : 1. .... 2. ....

5. According to Sarah what will the project's major drawback be?

....

6. What would the best solution be for Joan? ....

Je me situe par rapport au CECRL

Questions	Quand j'écoute cette interview, je peux :		☺	😐	☹
1	comprendre des informations précises simples.	A2			
2	comprendre le point essentiel de la discussion.	A2			
3	comprendre globalement le point de vue des personnes interviewées.	B1			
4-5-6	comprendre les points principaux des arguments de chaque personne.	B1			

COMPRÉHENSION DE L'ÉCRIT

Comprendre un récit

1. Where did Timothy go? .... What for? .... When? ....
2. What was the weather like when he arrived? (one adjective) ....
3. Use one adjective to describe the streets of London: .... New York : ....
4. How long did he stay in London? ....
5. Where did Timothy skate most of the time in London? ....
6. When it was dangerous, where did he skate? ....
7. "hassled" (l. 10) means: ☐ *renversé.* ☐ *embêté.* ☐ *applaudi.*
8. In London Timothy was surprised because he was not...

   a. .... b. often .... c. ....

Je me situe par rapport au CECRL

Questions	Lorsque je lis ce récit, je peux :		☺	😐	☹
1	en comprendre le sujet principal.	A2			
2-3-4	trouver une information particulière.	A2			
5-6-7	en comprendre l'essentiel.	B1			
8	réunir des informations provenant de différentes parties du récit.	B1			

Unit 8
page 123

LISTENER'S CORNER
Texting :)

LISTENING COMPREHENSION

CD 3/ 16-18

1 Akiria

A. What do most teenagers do on their cell phones today?

☐ they talk ☐ they text each other ☐ they play games

B. What do the following acronyms mean?

1. **lol:** laugh .... **2. brb:** be ....

C. How many text messages does Akiria often send in a day? ....

D. True or false? (Justify with words from the interview.)

1. T F According to Akiria, teens who say they can live without their cell phones don't tell the truth.

....

2. T F She says sending condolences through text messages is a good idea. ....
3. T F She thinks teens communicate in a way adults can't understand. ....

2 Sarah

E. Sarah decided to: ☐ stop texting her friends for a week. ☐ stop using her cell phone for a week.

F. Complete the sentences. (one blank = one word)

1. Each day I felt like something was .... – the same way .... drinkers feel without their morning ....
2. I longed for the feel of (*j'avais très envie de ressentir*) the .... underneath my ....

G. Sarah's week of no texting was: ☐ a success. ☐ a failure.

H. What were the consequences of no texting for Sarah?

☐ She stopped receiving texts. ☐ She missed plans. ☐ She lost some of her friends.
☐ She decided she would never deprive herself of texting again.

I. Sarah concludes that: texting makes her life .... and is .... of who she is.

3 Professor Christopher Brown

J. What is text messaging usually blamed for?

☐ having a negative impact on writing skills. ☐ costing a lot of money.
☐ being addictive. ☐ using phonetic spelling.
☐ preventing kids from doing their schoolwork. ☐ using no punctuation signs.

K. Professor Brown: ☐ **agrees** ☐ **disagrees with these criticisms.**

L. Why? (one blank = one word)

1. Most students don't use colloquial (*familier*) speech when addressing adults: they use .... – oriented and grammatically – .... speech.
2. Professor Brown believes that they can make the same distinction betweeen .... speech and the real English ....

TEXT 1
To kiss or not to kiss?

READING COMPREHENSION

A. Find three different verbs meaning: ***serrer (dans ses bras)***

1. ………… 2. ………… 3. …………

B. Find the equivalents of the following words:

1. *client :* ………… 3. *lèvre :* …………

2. *règle :* ………… 4. *joue :* …………

C. Use the formation of the following words to guess their meaning:

1. handshake (l. 3) ………… 2. employee (l. 8) …………

3. friendliness (l. 16) ………… 4. misinterpretation (l. 21) …………

5. exceedingly (l. 26) ………… 6. minefield (l. 35) …………

D. Traduisez ce groupe nominal en commençant par le dernier élément :

the firm, old-fashioned let's-keep-our-distance-thank-you handshake (l. 1): …………

…………

E. What is the rule concerning greeting in business circles in the UK nowadays? (Quote.)

…………

F. True or false? Justify by quoting from the text.

1. [T] [F] Social kissing has never been a way of greeting in Great Britain. …………

…………

2. [T] [F] In France, the rules concerning social kissing are easy to understand.

…………

3. [T] [F] Nowadays in Great Britain the greeting rules have become simple. …………

PRATIQUER LA GRAMMAIRE

Le comparatif et superlatif des adjectifs → Précis grammatical 25B, C, D

G. Complétez en mettant l'adjectif au comparatif de supériorité (>), au comparatif d'infériorité (<) ou au superlatif (+).

1. *It was much (easy) in the old days.* (>) …………
2. *You'll feel (good) after talking to him.* (>) …………
3. *It's (good) thing you have ever done.* (+) …………
4. *Isn't a handshake (embarrassing) than a kiss on the lips?* (<) …………
5. *It is (ambiguous) than a handshake.* (>) …………
6. *It is (complicated) decision I've ever had to face.* (+) …………
7. *Even at (busy) of times, I don't work as much as you do.* (+) …………
8. *I have never seen anything (bad).* (>) …………
9. *It's (big) mistake I've ever made.* (+) …………
10. *She is (stupid) than I thought.* (<) …………

TEXT 2

Generation clash

READING COMPREHENSION

1 Part one

A. When does the scene take place? Justify your answer.

☐ In the morning. ☐ In the evening. ☐ In the middle of the night. ....

B. Why is Linda in bed? Justify by quoting from the text.

☐ She is sick. ☐ She is depressed. ☐ She is tired. ☐ She wants to have a rest.

....

C. What are her plans for the night? ....

D. True or false? Justify your answer by quoting from the text.

T F Linda expected her mother to be angry because she was neither reading nor studying.

....

E. Use the context to guess the meaning of:

1. mildly (l. 9): ☐ *doucement* ☐ *gaiement* ☐ *sèchement*
2. grudgingly (l. 10): ☐ *gentiment* ☐ *à contrecœur* ☐ *joyeusement*
3. qualify (l. 11): ☐ *se qualifier* ☐ *obtenir un diplôme* ☐ *être sélectionné*
4. let (l. 12): ☐ *repeindre* ☐ *louer* ☐ *vendre*

F. What does the mother plan to do? Quote the text.

....

G. "Your ... father is unlikely to want to support the project" (l. 14) means:

Your father ☐ will probably agree. ☐ will probably disagree with the project.

H. What does Clara hope? Explain in your own words.

....

2 Part two

I. Quote the expression indicating that Linda would neither like to study nor to work next year:

....

J. Trouver les équivalents anglais des mots ou expressions suivantes :

1. *ce n'est pas la peine de t'en prendre à moi :* ....
2. *travailler comme un esclave pour gagner sa vie :* ....
3. *s'occuper de ses affaires :* ....
4. *décharger :* ....
5. *un orphelin affamé :* ....

K. Whose life is compared to Linda's? ....

L. **What is Linda unhappy about?**

- ☐ Her parents are divorced.
- ☐ Her mother works too much.
- ☐ Her mother drinks too much.
- ☐ Her father is marrying a young woman.
- ☐ Her mother blames her for not finding a job.
- ☐ Her mother makes her feel guilty.
- ☐ Her mother has forgotten that she agreed Linda would be a student.

Ten words to remember

Find the equivalents of these words in the text (in the right order) and learn them by heart.

1. *se préparer :* ....
2. *santé :* ....
3. *manque :* ....
4. *gagner (de l'argent) :* ....
5. *louer :* ....
6. *se demander :* ....
7. *en fait :* ....
8. *esclave :* ....
9. *affamé :* ....
10. *orphelin :* ....

ENRICHIR SON LEXIQUE – Les mots dérivés en *-ly*

A. **Complétez le tableau.**

Mots du texte en *-ly*	Nature	Traduction	Base	Nature
1. ***early*** (l. 4)	(ici) adverbe	tôt		
2. ***surely*** (l. 7)	adverbe	sûrement	*sure*	adjectif
3.	....	....	....	....
4.	....	....	....	....
5.	....	....	....	....
6.	....	....	....	....
7.	....	....	....	....
8.	....	....	....	....

B. **Déduisez une règle :** En anglais, de très nombreux .... se forment à partir d' .... en ajoutant le suffixe *-ly*.

C. **Certains adverbes terminés en *-ly* posent des problèmes de traduction car la base peut mettre sur une fausse piste ou la dérivation n'existe pas en français. Traduisez ou cherchez la traduction des adverbes suivants.**

1. *presently:* ....
2. *eventually:* ....
3. *hardly:* ....
4. *definitely:* ....
5. *lastly:* ....
6. *unexpectedly:* ....
7. *lately:* ....
8. *angrily:* ....
9. *expensively:* ....
10. *convincingly:* ....

D. **Certains adjectifs se terminent également en *-ly*. Traduisez ceux-ci.**

1. *friendly:* ....
2. *lonely:* ....
3. *deadly:* ....
4. *daily:* ....

E. **Déduisez de vos réponses précédentes la traduction des mots suivants.**

1. *viril:* ....
2. *hebdomadaire:* ....
3. *mensuel:* ....
4. *annuel:* ....

PRATIQUER LA GRAMMAIRE

1 *HAVE SOMETHING DONE* → Précis grammatical 36B

A. Lisez l'énoncé ci-dessous et répondez aux questions a, b et c.

"...I was thinking of ***having a second bathroom built****"* (l. 13)

a. Soulignez la proposition (**1** ou **2**) qui exprime le mieux le sens de la structure en gras.

1. La mère envisage qu'une deuxième salle de bains soit construite.

2. La mère envisage de construire elle-même une deuxième salle de bains.

b. *"built"* est-il : **1.** un prétérit ou **2.** un participe passé à sens passif ? : ....

c. Traduisez l'énoncé. ....

....

B. Traduisez à l'aide la structure *have something done*.

1. Nous avons fait changer la serrure *(the lock)* le mois dernier.

....

2. Je ferai réparer ma voiture la semaine prochaine.

....

3. Elle fait laver *(clean)* sa voiture une fois par semaine *(once a week)*.

....

4. Il s'est fait couper les cheveux hier.

....

2 *'D : HAD OU WOULD* → Précis grammatical 8, 17

C. Écrivez *'D* sous forme pleine (*HAD* ou *WOULD*) à la suite de chaque énoncé et indiquez également si la forme verbale soulignée est : a. un conditionnel ou **b.** un *pluperfect*

1. *"Sorry, I didn't think <u>you'd be</u> in bed this early."* (l. 4) ....

2. *She told her me <u>she'd had</u> a very bad day.* ....

3. *I knew <u>she'd come back</u> the night before.* ....

4. *<u>She'd probably come back</u> if only you asked her.* ....

3 Les pronoms réciproques et réfléchis → Précis grammatical 23C, D

D. Indiquez si le(s) pronom(s) en gras :

a. renvoie(nt) aux mêmes personnes que le sujet de la phrase (pronom réfléchi).

b. exprime(nt) un échange entre deux personnes (pronom réciproque).

Écrivez a ou b à la suite de chaque énoncé, puis traduisez.

1. *"My parents hate* ***each other****."* (l. 24-25) : ....

2. *They introduced* ***themselves*** *to the group.* ....

E. Complétez avec *each other* ou *themselves*.

1. *Did they enjoy* ....?

2. *The two brothers never write to* ....

3. *The two kids love* .... *very much.*

CHECK YOUR SKILLS

COMPRÉHENSION DE L'ORAL

Your CD 46-47 | CD 3 29-30

Comprendre une interview

1. First speaker's name: .... **Age:** .... **. He is ☐ for or ☐ against brands.**

2. Complete the sentences with words from the interview.

a. The speaker does not understand why brands should be reserved for ....

b. He loves wearing .... and classy clothes.

c. He thinks that buying brands is better than buying ....

d. He does not mind his parents calling him a ....

3. Tick the names of the famous people mentioned by the speaker.

☐ Lord Durham ☐ Oscar Wilde ☐ Lord Byron ☐ Oscar Peterson ☐ David Bowie ☐ David Beckham

4. Explain in your own words why the speaker mentions these people.

....

5. Second Speaker's name: .... **Age:** .... **. She is ☐ for or ☐ against brands.**

6. True or false? Circle the correct answer and justify with keywords.

a. T F She thinks brands are essential to style. ....

b. T F She loves expensive jeans. ....

c. T F She wants to dress like American stars. ....

7. What is the speaker's personal motto (*devise*)? ....

Je me situe par rapport au CECRL

Questions	Lorsque j'écoute cette interview, je peux :		☺	😐	☹
1-3-5	comprendre des informations précises simples ainsi que le sujet général.	A2			
2-6	en comprendre les points principaux.	B1			
4	comprendre les arguments utilisés par le locuteur.	B1			
7	comprendre le point de vue du locuteur.	B1			

INTERACTION ORALE

Prendre part à une discussion

Je me situe par rapport au CECRL

Quand je prends part à une discussion, je peux :		☺	😐	☹
justifier très simplement mes opinions ou mes actes si je m'y suis préparé avant.	A2			
exprimer mon accord ou mon désaccord.	A2			
demander de répéter en termes simples si je ne comprends pas.	A2			
sans préparation, justifier brièvement mes opinions ou mes actes.	B1			
expliquer pourquoi je suis en désaccord avec un point de vue qui a été exprimé.	B1			
interrompre poliment mon interlocuteur quand je ne suis pas d'accord ou quand je n'ai pas compris.	B1			
m'exprimer autrement si mon interlocuteur ne me comprend pas.	B1			

Écouter et prononcer

1 Symboles phonétiques

A. Prononcez les mots suivants et cochez la transcription phonétique correcte de chacun. Vérifiez à l'écoute.

1. *breakfast*: □ /'brekfæst/ □ /'brekfəst/
2. *chocolate*: □ /'tʃɒklɪt/ □ /'tʃɒkəleɪt/
3. *father*: □ /'fɑːðə/ □ /'fæðə/
4. *photographer*: □ /fə'tɒgrəfɪ/ □ /fə'tɒgrəfə/
5. *completely*: □ /kəm'pliːtlɪ/ □ /kɒm'pliːtlɪ/
6. *useful*: □ /juːs'fʊl/ □ /'juːsfʊl/
7. *character*: □ /'kærɪktə/ □ /'kɪrræktə/
8. *society*: □ /sə'saɪətɪ/ □ /sɒ'sɪətɪ/

2 Accent de mot

B. Prononcez puis écrivez les mots correspondant aux transcriptions phonétiques. (L'accent de mot n'est pas indiqué.) Entourez la syllabe accentuée. Vérifiez à l'écoute.

1. /rɪəlaɪz/: ....
2. /səksiːd/: ....
3. /spektækjʊlə/: ....
4. /dɪtektɪv/: ....
5. /ðəmselvz/: ....
6. /bɪkɒz/: ....
7. /kəmpɛə/: ....
8. /fɒləʊ/: ....
9. /nɒlɪdʒ/: ....

C. Prononcez les mots suivants et entourez la syllabe accentuée. Vérifiez à l'écoute.

1. beautiful
2. education
3. September
4. Japan
5. passenger
6. adjective
7. important
8. identity
9. before
10. vegetable
11. interesting
12. international
13. tomato
14. Canada
15. shampoo
16. arrive

3 Réduction des voyelles

D. Prononcez puis écrivez les mots correspondant aux transcriptions phonétiques. Barrez la (les) voyelle(s) orthographique(s) réduites. Vérifiez à l'écoute.

1. /bə'nɑːnə/: ....
2. /'pɪktʃə/: ....
3. /'vɪlɪdʒ/: ....
4. /'sæləd/: ....
5. /ə'gen/: ....
6. /kən'sɪdə/: ....
7. /ə'bɪlɪtɪ/: ....
8. /'faʊntɪn/: ....
9. /'ɒksfəd/: ....
10. /sək'ses/: ....
11. /əd'mɪt/: ....
12. /ˌdemə'krætɪk/: ....
13. /'dʒenərəl/: ....
14. /baɪ'ɒgrəfɪ/: ....
15. /əd'vɑːntɪdʒ/: ....

E. Lisez cette phrase et barrez les voyelles orthographiques réduites. Vérifiez à l'écoute.

I suppose you've forgotten to explain to the police about that famous doctor!

4 Prononciation de la marque *-ed*

F. Prononcez les mots suivants, puis classez-les dans la case appropriée en fonction de la prononciation de la marque *-ed* : [d], [t] ou [ɪd]. Vérifiez à l'écoute.

tried – looked – added – explained – laughed – tested – shocked – rented – shared – started – rushed – mixed – landed – obliged – hoped – pulled – imagined – researched – pleased – dressed

/d/	
/t/	
/ɪd/	

5 Repérer les liaisons

G. Écoutez l'exemple et observez les liaisons. Marquez ensuite les liaisons qui doivent être faites dans les autres phrases. Vérifiez vos réponses à l'écoute.

Exemple : *When‿I noticed‿her‿in‿a pub, I went‿over to talk.*

1. *We're living in a small town. There are no buses after eight.*
2. *Can I have a piece of apple pie? And a cup of tea?*
3. *I must have made a mistake when I asked him to come immediately.*
4. *There's a man at the door, shall I let him in?*
5. *I'll ask Peter and Ann to come over as soon as possible.*

6 Intonation

H1. Vous allez entendre huit phrases. Repérez l'intonation montante ou descendante à la fin de chaque phrase puis écrivez la flèche correcte (↗ ou ↘) dans la case correspondante.

H2. Vous allez entendre les mêmes phrases que dans l'exercice H1. Repérez le type de phrase (affirmative, négative, etc.) et cochez la case correspondante dans le tableau.

		1	2	3	4	5	6	7	8
H1	Intonation (↗ ou ↘)								
H2	Phrase affirmative								
	Phrase négative								
	Énumération								
	Ordre								
	Yes/No question								
	Wh- question								
	Tag (vraie question)								
	Tag (fausse question)								

7 Repérer les groupes de sens

I. Marquez les groupes de sens dans les phrases ci-dessous à l'aide des symboles / (pause courte) ou // (pause longue).

1. *He says he will, to tell the truth.*
2. *And so I spent that whole long afternoon in the red room asking myself why I had to suffer and why life was so unfair.*
3. *For me, the first message I remember came when I was eight or nine.*
4. *These things have little to do with what we were told was important in school.*

Compréhension de l'oral

1 Faire des hypothèses sur le sens global du document

CD 4 24

Exercice 1 Écoutez le début d'une pièce radiophonique.

1. Quels indices sonores vous permettent de dire où l'action se déroule ?

....

....

2. Quelle atmosphère est donnée par le ton de la voix et la musique ?

....

2 Repérer et mémoriser

CD 4 25-27

Exercice 2 Écoutez l'interview de Thomas.

1. Repérez 4 mots porteurs de sens :

....

2. Selon vous à quelle question Thomas a-t-il répondu ?

☐ *Could you explain what being a punk means for you?*

☐ *Do you like watching animal documentaries on TV?*

☐ *Do you think that men and women are treated equally?*

Exercice 3 Vous allez entendre dix noms propres. Vous devriez en reconnaître au moins six :

1. .... 6. ....
2. .... 7. ....
3. .... 8. ....
4. .... 9. ....
5. .... 10. ....

Exercice 4 Écrivez les nombres, les pourcentages, les dates, et les numéros de téléphone que vous entendez.

1. .... 4. .... 7. ....
2. .... 5. .... 8. ....
3. .... 6. .... 9. ....

3 Classer, relier et hiérarchiser

CD 4 28

Exercice 5 Écoutez cet extrait de *Youth Radio* et répondez aux questions :

a. *How old is Erin?* .... *Where is she from? Country:* .... *City:* ....

b. *When did the discussion take place?*
☐ *during the break* (récréation) ☐ *during history class* ☐ *before going to school*

c. *What dates does the teacher mention? What do they refer to?*

1. ....

2. ....

d. *What date does one student mention? What does it refer to?*

....

e. *What other date is mentioned? What does it refer to?*

....

4 Synthétiser

Exercice 5 **Ré-écoutez cet enregistrement et expliquez en français le message du narrateur.**

....

....

5 Comprendre un reportage

Exercice 6 **Vous allez écouter un reportage du *Guardian*. Suivez la démarche proposée dans votre manuel (p. 157-158) et dans les exercices précédents afin de le comprendre au mieux.**

A. Première écoute

1. Quels indices sonores vous permettent de dire dans quel lieu le reportage se déroule ? Répondez en français.

....

B. Écoutes suivantes. Répondez en anglais :

2. ***In which city is the restaurant located?*** ☐ *Brighton* ☐ *Bristol* ☐ *Brenton*

3. ***The exact address is not given because: (two answers)***
☐ *the reporter thinks it is not important.* ☐ *the owners are afraid of having too many customers.*
☐ *the owners are worried about being shut down.* ☐ *it is not a good restaurant.*

4. ***Complete (one blank = one word)***
An .... *collective is* .... *this building and using it as a restaurant.*

5. ***How many nights have they opened up the restaurant?*** ....

6. ***What will happen afterwards? The owners will:***
☐ *retire.* ☐ *go on holiday.*
☐ *move to another place.* ☐ *change jobs.*

7. ***What sort of food do they serve?***
☐ *British food* ☐ *Canadian food*
☐ *Caledonian food* ☐ *Columbian food*

8. ***What is the place decorated with? (four answers)***
☐ *flowers and plants* ☐ *dark wood stairs* ☐ *velvet curtains* ☐ *modern paintings*
☐ *black and white photographs* ☐ *candles* ☐ *antique furniture* ☐ *wood sculptures*

9. ***Contrary to other restaurants, you are allowed to*** .... ***in this restaurant.***

10. ***Price:*** *It's not for* .... *as the customer* .... *what to pay at the end of the meal.*

11. ***"the rebel restaurant is completely booked out" means:***
☐ *There are no tables available.* ☐ *The restaurant is about to close down.*
☐ *There are very few customers in this restaurant.*

12. ***The journalist sounds:*** ☐ *indifferent* ☐ *enthusiastic* ☐ *sceptical*

C. Rendez-compte de ce que vous avez compris.

13. Résumez les points principaux de cet enregistrement et expliquez pourquoi le journaliste a fait un reportage sur ce lieu. (oralement et en français)

Compréhension de l'écrit

1 Anticipation

A. Associez un sous-titre (a, b ou c) à chacun des titres de presse suivants.

1. *2,000 MORE WIND TURBINES IN COUNTRYSIDE* ....
2. *FINAL STAR WARS BEARS MESSAGE FOR AMERICA* ....
3. *SHE WORKS, HE DOESN'T* ....

a. *The number of American families in which the woman is the only wage earner is growing.*
b. *Minister promises numbers will double to generate 10 percent of UK energy within 5 years.*
c. *George Lucas wins trophy – and hopes his epic will awaken US to democracy in peril.*

B. Associez à chaque titre de presse le résumé de l'article (a, b ou c) correspondant.

1. *A LESSON E-LEARNED* ....
2. *FIVE-YEAR-OLDS GIVEN MOBILES* ....
3. *EMPLOYEES FEAR FLEXITIME WILL HURT CAREER* ....

a. Malgré les risques, des millions de très jeunes enfants utilisent des téléphones portables.
b. De plus en plus d'employés suivent des cours de formation professionnelle sur Internet.
c. En Grande-Bretagne, les horaires à la carte attirent de moins en moins de travailleurs.

2 Compréhension globale

C. Lisez l'extrait suivant sans vous arrêter aux mots inconnus et répondez en quelques mots (en anglais) aux questions 1 à 7.

Emma Woodhouse, handsome, clever, and rich, with a comfortable home and happy disposition, seemed to unite some of the best blessings of existence and had lived nearly twenty-one years in the world with very little to distress her.

She was the younger of the two daughters of a most affectionate, indulgent father, and had, in consequence of her sister's marriage, been mistress of his house from a very early period. Her mother had died too long ago for her to have more than an indistinct remembrance of her caresses and her place had been supplied by an excellent woman as governess, who had fallen little short of a mother in affection.

Sixteen years had Miss Taylor been in the family, less as a governess than a friend, very fond of both daughters, but particularly of Emma. Between them it was more the intimacy of sisters. The mildness of Miss Taylor's temper had hardly allowed her to impose any restraint and they had been living together as friend and friend very mutually attached, and Emma doing just what she liked, highly esteeming Miss Taylor's judgment, but directed chiefly by her own.

Jane AUSTEN, *Emma*

1. *Main characters:* ....
2. *Secondary characters:* ....
3. *Miss Taylor's job:* ....
4. *How long?* ....
5. *Emma's age:* ....
6. *Emma's character:* ☐ *submissive* ☐ *determined* *l affectionate*
7. *Relationship between Emma and Miss Taylor:* ....

3 Compréhension détaillée

D. Soulignez les mots de liaison dans les extraits suivants et traduisez-les.

1. *Since 1995, the obesity rate among French children has doubled, from 6% to 12%. Moreover, the percentage of obese adults jumped from 37% to 42% between 1997 and 2003.*

2. *As soon as I arrived I made an attempt to find my host. However, the two or three people of whom I asked his whereabouts denied vehemently any knowledge of his movements.*

3. *Shadow did not believe in anything he could not see. Yet, he could feel disaster hovering above the prison in those final weeks, just as he had felt it in the days before the robbery.*

Mots de liaison ....

....

E. Lisez l'extrait suivant et trouvez les référents des pronoms soulignés.

America, Stefan believed, was the country where **(1)** people brought about changes instead of resisting them **(2)**. But his parents didn't want to listen when he **(3)** read to them **(4)** about immigrants who **(5)** earned fortunes; they **(6)** didn't know that America had grafted itself **(7)** to his mind so tenaciously that he **(8)** had dreams of it **(9)** every night.

Ursula HEGI, *The Vision of Emma Blau*

1. .... 4. .... 7. ....

2. .... 5. .... 8. ....

3. .... 6. .... 9. ....

F. Tous les *that* (subordonnées en *that* ou pronoms relatifs) ont été supprimés dans ces deux extraits. Mettez une croix aux endroits où ils pourraient être placés.

1. *A recent survey found 86 per cent of Britons believe fathers should be more closely involved with their children. But research shows many stressed-out working fathers struggle to find six minutes a day to talk and play, one-to-one, with their children.*

2. *American researchers say their findings prove television and video games have a direct influence on violent behaviour. They suggest there are potential benefits in reducing the time children are allowed to spend on these activities.*

G. Il y a dix groupes nominaux complexes dans cet extrait. Soulignez-les et encadrez le nom principal dans chaque groupe.

The Royal Air Force has about 20 female combat pilots and roughly the same number of fast jet navigators. Women, however, are not allowed to serve on submarines, or as Royal Marine Commando troops. Nor are they allowed in the Royal Air Force Regiment, which provides combat units for airfield defence. The Army's 7,400 women can apply for 70 per cent of the posts available, many of which would take them near to the front line, such as forward artillery observer and combat medic.

The Daily Telegraph

4 Mots inconnus : nature

H. Lisez le texte suivant et trouvez la nature de chaque mot souligné : nom, adjectif, adverbe ou verbe. Complétez le tableau ci-dessous.

On the morning of the fourth, after an anxious and most <u>perilous</u> but <u>safe</u> journey, I found myself in the big city of New York, a free man. For the moment, the dreams of my <u>youth</u> and the hopes of my <u>manhood</u> were completely <u>fulfilled</u>. The <u>bonds</u> that had <u>held</u> me to "old master" were broken. No man now had a right to call me his slave or <u>assert</u> <u>mastery</u> over me. A new world had opened upon me. It was a time of joyous excitement which words can but <u>tamely</u> describe.

Frederick DOUGLASS, *Narrative of the Life of Frederick Douglass, an American Slave*

Nom	Adjectif	Adverbe	Verbe

I. Lisez le texte suivant et trouvez la nature de chaque mot manquant : nom, adjectif, adverbe ou verbe. Écrivez le chiffre correspondant dans la bonne case du tableau.

The hour passed **(1)**. He could hear her watching **(2)**. She **(3)** as soon as it was eight o'clock, with two **(4)** and a glass of water. Paul **(5)** lifted himself up on to his **(6)** when she **(7)** on his bed. "At last I got your **(8)** book, two days ago," she told him. *Misery's Child*. I **(9)** it. It's as **(10)** as all the others. Better, in fact. It's the best."

Stephen KING, *Misery*

Nom	Adjectif	Adverbe	Verbe

5 Mots inconnus : transparence

J. Lisez le texte suivant et aidez-vous des mots transparents soulignés pour résumer le passage brièvement en français.

There are no <u>services</u> in Kibera – no running water, no rubbish <u>collection</u>, <u>virtually</u> no <u>electricity</u>, not a single flush <u>toilet</u>. Kibera is only one of about a hundred slums in Nairobi, and it is by no means the worst. More than half of Nairobi's three <u>million</u> people are <u>packed</u> into these <u>immensely</u> squalid <u>zones</u>, which together <u>occupy</u> only about 1.5% of the <u>city</u>'s land.

Bill BRYSON, *African Diary*

Résumé : ....

....

6 Mots inconnus : formation

K. Chaque mot souligné dans ces extraits est un mot dérivé. Trouvez sa formation (base, préfixe, suffixe), sa nature (nom, adjectif, adverbe, verbe) et sa traduction probable. (cf. l'exemple avec *disability* dans le tableau.)

1. *She <u>unbuttoned</u> her coat <u>slowly</u>, looked at her baby and whispered, "I love you."*
2. *She raised her veil as she spoke, and we could see that she was in a <u>pitiable</u> state of agitation, her face all grey, with <u>restless</u> eyes, like those of some <u>hunted</u> animal.*
3. *The man took his eyes off Steve Peterson and studied the girl <u>thoughtfully</u>.*

	Base	Préfixe/suffixe	Nature	Traduction
disability	*able*	*dis- + -ity*	nom	incapacité
unbuttoned				
slowly				
pitiable				
restless				
hunted				
thoughtfully				

L. Chaque mot souligné dans ces extraits est un mot composé. Trouvez comment il a été formé, sa nature (nom ou adjectif) et sa traduction probable.

1. *Nameless villages and invisible hills lurked in rain-swept darkness beyond the headlights, but I knew that this unknown road would lead me sooner or later to the motorway.*
2. *Hold fast to dreams / For if dreams die / Life is a broken-winged bird / That cannot fly.*
3. *I tried twice more before the door-handle turned and a shy-looking woman peeked her head.*

	Formation	Nature	Traduction
rain-swept			
headlights			
motorway			
broken-winged			
door-handle			
shy-looking			

7 Mots inconnus : contexte

M. Servez-vous du contexte pour cocher la bonne traduction des mots soulignés.

When mother was busy, I worked on by myself, trying to make out (1) words whenever I came across (2) them. I used to try and spell out (3) the names of the objects around me at home, like fire, picture, dog, door, chair, and so on. I was very proud of myself when I had mastered a new word and could write it down for mother to show her what a great scholar (4) I was.

Christie BROWN, *My Left Foot*

1. *make out:* ☐ fabriquer ☐ rédiger ☐ déchiffrer ☐ présenter ☐ remplacer
2. *came across:* ☐ tombais sur ☐ traversais ☐ repassais ☐ signalais ☐ suivais
3. *spell out:* ☐ hurler ☐ expliquer ☐ déchirer ☐ épeler ☐ faire semblant de lire
4. *scholar:* ☐ boursier ☐ professeur ☐ collégien ☐ lycéen ☐ érudit

N. Servez-vous du contexte pour trouver la bonne traduction des mots soulignés.

Thanks to a booming (1) economy and an unusual collaboration between labor (2) and industry, Las Vegas has become a paradise for people like Ms. Diaz: unskilled (3) newcomers, many of them immigrants. In Las Vegas, unlike most other American cities, dishwashers (4) or hotel janitors (5) can easily gain a foothold (6) in the middle class.

The New York Times

1. .... 3. .... 5. ....

2. .... 4. .... 6. ....

Expression orale en continu

1 Raconter

A. Résumez un film.

Vous racontez le film de votre choix à un camarade. Celui-ci vous impose d'utiliser cinq mots de liaison (voir Manuel pages 162 et 163).

N'oubliez pas qu'un bon résumé répond généralement aux questions suivantes :

Where? When? Who? What? Why?

B. Racontez la vie d'une célébrité.

1. Choisissez un personnage célèbre aujourd'hui disparu et préparez une présentation orale des éléments les plus pertinents de sa biographie.
2. Vous présenterez ce personnage à la classe sans en révéler le nom, à vos camarades de le trouver.

N'oubliez pas d'utiliser les mots de liaison afin de donner de la cohérence à votre présentation.

2 Présenter, expliquer, argumenter

C. Lisez ce début d'article et parlez du sujet en vous aidant des questions.

Can charity change the world?
The concept of charity – generous actions to help the poor, ill or helpless – is an ancient one, and the practice of providing for the needy has always been deeply rooted in religion, in society, and more recently, in governments...
Not everyone agrees that charity is the solution to the world' s problems.

Speakeasy, Jan. Feb. 2010

1. *What is the origin of this document?*
2. *Pick out a few keywords and explain what the whole article is about.*
3. *What information will you probably find in the article?*
4. *What is your opinion: do you think charity is the solution to the world's problems?*

D. Lisez ces titres de journaux, imaginez puis présentez le contenu des articles.

Pour pouvoir en parler il vous faut, bien sûr, d'abord comprendre ces titres.

Rappel : Les titres de journaux sont souvent difficiles à comprendre.

Dans ces deux cas, il vous faut :
– repérer d'abord le verbe qui est le pivot de la phrase.
– repérer et analyser les noms composés en commençant par le dernier élément.

School truancy[1] rises to highest recorded level

Earth Hour
Climate change campaigners urge[2] global switch-off

1. absentéisme
2. demander avec insistance

3 Décrire et analyser une image

E. *Picture 1*

1. *What kind of document is it?*
2. *Describe the situation.*
3. *Describe the various characters and imagine their feelings.*
4. *Imagine the reason(s) why the man has been stopped.*

You can use the following words:
film still (*image de film*) – patrolman – chauffeur /ˈʃəʊfə/ – driving licence – registration certificate – check – driving offence – go over the speed limit – racial prejudice

F. *Picture 2*

1. *What kind of document does this photo certainly illustrate?*
2. *What is its main topic?*
3. *Describe the document.*
4. *What are these people protesting against?*
5. *What does the tape on their mouths symbolize?*
6. *Imagine the rest of the slogan in the foreground.*

You can use the following words:
demonstration – activist – placard /ˈplækɑːd/ – denounce – slogan – be gagged (*être bâilloné*) – silence (*faire taire*)

4 Décrire et analyser une publicité

G. *Picture 3 :* indiquez à l'aide de flèches où se trouvent les divers éléments dans la publicité ci-dessous.

Catchphrase

Picture

Product

Logo

Slogan

Brand name

H. *Picture 4 :* décrivez et analysez la publicité ci-dessous en vous aidant des questions.

1. *Describe the ad.*
2. *What is the aim of this ad?*
3. *Who is the target?*
4. *Do you feel concerned by the issue raised in this ad?*
5. *How do you personally react to this ad? Why?*

You can use the following words:
green – environment – recycle – be aware of – re-use – protect – pollute

Interaction orale

1 Expressions utiles

Assurez-vous que vous connaissez les expressions nécessaires pour discuter et débattre.

Remplissez-le tableau suivant sans vous aider de votre manuel dans un premier temps. Complétez-le avec votre manuel si nécessaire.

Gap-fillers	• .... • .... • .... • .... • ....
S'assurer que l'interlocuteur suit la conversation	• .... • .... • ....
Indiquer que l'on suit la conversation	• .... • .... • .... • ....
Convaincre	• .... • .... • .... • .... • ....
Demander des précisions	• .... • .... • .... • ....
Exprimer son désaccord	• .... • .... • .... • .... • ....
Interrompre poliment	• .... • .... • ....

2 Conversation

Student A: You are a British teenager and you have just arrived in France. You ask student B for advice about the places where you can have fun.

Student B: You are a French teenager and you help student A to enjoy his /her stay in France.

3 Interview

Student A: You are a rock / sports / film star and you accept to be interviewed about your life.

Student B: You are a young journalist and interview a famous star: you ask him / her questions about his/her childhood, youth, beginning, first success, difficulties,...

4 Discussion contradictoire

For or against banning cell phones on public transportation?

Remplissez le tableau avec des arguments pour et contre. Puis vous défendrez l'une des positions. Vous pourrez ensuite alterner les rôles.

For	*Against*

5 Débat

1. **Lisez l'extrait suivant et préparez-vous à débattre.**

Should animals be kept in zoos?
For many people, the zoo is a source of childhood amazement and fond memories: swinging monkeys, laughing hyenas and growling tigers. Conservationists say zoos advance their educational and preservationist efforts, but others see zoos as prisons where innocent creatures are unjustly held captive.

2. **Répartissez les rôles : présentateur, équipe pour, équipe contre.**
Chaque équipe prépare au moins trois arguments et s'apprête à réfuter les arguments de l'équipe adverse.

For	*Against*

Expression écrite

1 Rédiger des phrases correctes

A. Lisez les mots-clés suivants, qui proviennent d'une dépêche d'agence. Utilisez-les ensuite pour écrire un court article de quatre phrases sur papier libre. Faites des phrases complètes et tenez compte des conseils donnés ci-dessous.

1. last week – 19 migrant workers – hiding in truck – found dead – not far – El Paso – Texas
2. past five years – 2000 Mexican migrants – wanted – cross US border – died
3. drowned – Rio Grande – died of sun exposure – desert – froze to death – mountains
4. ready – risk their lives – get – lowest-paying jobs – United States

- Phrase **1** : introduisez une phrase relative et mettez un verbe à la voix passive.
- Phrase **2** : introduisez une phrase relative et conjuguez un verbe au *present perfect*.
- Phrase **3** : introduisez des sujets et variez-les en évitant les pronoms personnels.
- Phrase **4** : introduisez un sujet de type général et une subordonnée de but.

2 Vérifier la ponctuation

B. Rétablissez la ponctuation dans ce passage, extrait de *Robinson Crusoe* (Daniel Defoe).

the poor creature was trembling he walked towards me slowly when he came close to me he knelt on the ground and kissed the earth I helped him to his feet the savage I had knocked down now began to move I pointed to him to show my savage that his enemy was not dead my savage spoke some words to me I did not understand them but I enjoyed listening to them they were the first words spoken to me by any human being for over twenty-five years my savage touched the sword at my side as if asking to use it I gave it to him and he ran to his enemy and cut off his head with one blow when he had done this he came back to me laughing and gave me my sword

3 Écrire une lettre

C. Lisez la lettre qu'Antonin a envoyée à la famille britannique qui l'a accueilli.

1. Soulignez les formules de politesse utilisées. Quel est le style de cette lettre ?

☐ formel ☐ semi-formel ☐ informel ☐ familier

Dear Mr and Mrs Smith,
I would like to thank you for letting me stay with you during the holidays. I really enjoyed myself and it was a great pleasure to stay with your family. I also discovered another culture and I am sure that staying with an English family broadened my horizons. My English has greatly improved and I am sure that my English teacher will notice it.
I am looking forward to seeing Steve over here. I am sure that we will have a wonderful time together. Best wishes to all of you.
Yours,
Antonin

2. Réécrivez cette lettre dans un style familier sur papier libre. Dans celle-ci, Antonin ne souhaite remercier que Steve. Utilisez les formes appropriées et les expressions suivantes : *thanks – have fun – have a good time – can't believe one's ears – must rush – can't wait to.*

4 Imaginer un récit

D. Racontez l'histoire suivante en 150-200 mots.

Paul, a young actor who has been unemployed for several months, has just had an appointment with Kent Marantino, a famous movie producer. After the interview, he tells one of his friends what happened.

1. Alternez narration et dialogue.

• Utilisez les temps de la narration : prétérit simple > actions ponctuelles ; prétérit *BE+ING* > description, action en déroulement.

• Variez les verbes introducteurs pour la partie dialoguée (voir Manuel, p. 169)

2. Ajoutez des mots de liaison en particulier ceux permettant de rendre compte de la chronologie des événements : *as soon as, first, then, finally, meanwhile...*

5 Rédiger un article de presse

E. Écrivez un article sur la carrière de Jude Law en prêtant attention aux formes verbales et en faisant des phrases complexes lorsque c'est possible.

Mots utiles : *run* (diriger) – *act / play / star in – rise to fame – win*

Jude LAW

- Date and place of birth: Dec. 29, 1972 – Lewisham, South London, UK.
- Parents' occupation: school teachers, now theatre company in France.
- First role at 12.
- 1990: gave up school at 17, first major role in TV soap *Families*.
- 1992: stage career: many plays in London, then on Broadway, NYC.
- 1997: screen career: *Gattaca*, *Midnight in the Garden of Good and Evil*.
- 1999: *The Talented Mr Ripley* (co-star Matt Damon)
- Since 1999: *Artificial Intelligence: A.I* (2001), *Cold Mountain* (2003), *Sherlock Holmes* (2009)
- 2003: divorced Sadie Frost (three children)
- Named "Sexiest man alive" by *People magazine* in 2004
- Awards: Honorary César (2007) – Several theatre awards – Many film nominations.

6 Rédiger un essai

Sujet : *Would you like to be famous? Explain why or why not.*

F. Introduire le sujet.

1. Choisissez l'introduction a, b ou c.

a. ☐ *Yes, I would really like to be famous because life must be wonderful when people recognize you in the street. That's why it would be interesting to weigh the pros and cons* (peser le pour et le contre) *of celebrity.*

b. ☐ *Nowadays, a lot of young people want to be famous because they're influenced by the media, so this is quite a topical* (d'actualité) *question. That's why it would be interesting to weigh the pros and cons of celebrity.*

c. ☐ *I think that in today's society a lot of people are famous for doing nothing in particular. That's why it would be interesting to weigh the pros and cons of celebrity.*

2. Justifiez votre choix brièvement : ....

....

G. Développement et conclusion : rassembler des idées et organiser un plan.

Remarque : Dans cet exercice, nous avons anticipé une réponse positive à la question posée dans le sujet. Il faut donc choisir un plan logique.

1. Soulignez les mots de liaison qui vont vous permettre d'ordonner et d'articuler les paragraphes. Assurez-vous que vous en connaissez le sens (voir Manuel, p. 162).

2. Ordonnez les phrases du tableau afin de construire votre développement en trois parties et trouver une conclusion. Écrivez ci-dessous les lettres correspondantes aux phrases, dans l'ordre logique.

- Développement
  - – Partie 1 (3 phrases) : ....
  - – Partie 2 (3 phrases) : ....
  - – Partie 3 (3 phrases) : ....
- Conclusion (2 phrases) : ....

a. Now, let us focus on the drawbacks (*inconvénients*) of fame.
b. First of all, we must bear in mind (*garder à l'esprit*) that it is common today to see a lot of ordinary people appear on TV, in reality shows for example.
c. To begin with, the main drawback is that you have no more privacy since famous people, whether they are in show business or not, are constantly in the public eye.
d. And even if they have no talent, these people soon become more famous than the greatest scientists.
e. Moreover, when you fight for a cause, you are definitely more effective and powerful if you are famous.
f. That's why I really think that this kind of celebrity is meaningless.
g. Last, but not least, if life is richer and more rewarding (*gratifiante*) when you are famous, why settle (*se contenter de*) for a boring and narrow (*étriquée*) existence?
h. One of these advantages is that fame is a visible sign of your success and can bring you respect, admiration and open doors for you.
i. For all these reasons, and as long as it is not an end in itself, but the consequence of an exceptional contribution to art, science, sport, politics or humanitarian work, I believe that there is every reason to be proud of being famous.
j. Furthermore, it will also be difficult for you to appreciate (*évaluer*) the sincerity of those who say they are your friends, unless you know them well.
k. And yet, we must acknowledge (*reconnaître*) that celebrity does have a lot of advantages.

7 Contrôler sa production

H. Chacune des phrases suivantes contient plusieurs erreurs. Soulignez ces erreurs et réécrivez les phrases en anglais correct.

1. *There had much people at the concert yesterday. It has been a concert very nice.*

....

2. *This american scientist works since two years on a mission secret. He told to anybody about his project.*

....

3. *They want that he works more at school because he have too much bad marks.*

....

4. *He think that everybody were happy after his birthday party.*

....

5. *He will must work more if he want to have a good job when he will be more old.*

....

6. *He love his neighbours's new car! He would to buy the same car than them.*

....

7. HARRY: *You think that he will can do it?* SALLY: *No, I think not. He is not enough strong!*

....

Notez la date et le titre de l'activité de compréhension orale que vous venez de faire, puis faites le point sur ce que vous êtes capable de faire.
Vous pourrez ainsi mesurer vos progrès tout au long de l'année et vous situer par rapport au niveau B1.

Compréhension de l'oral B1			**Je peux comprendre les points principaux d'une intervention.**			**Je peux comprendre les points de détail d'un message dans une intervention pas trop longue.**			**Je peux comprendre les arguments utilisés par le locuteur.**			**Je peux comprendre le point de vue du locuteur.**		
Date	**Titre de l'activité du manuel ou du fichier de l'élève**	**Page**	☺	😐	☹	☺	😐	☹	☺	😐	☹	☺	😐	☹
			☐	☐	☐	☐	☐	☐	☐	☐	☐	☐	☐	☐
			☐	☐	☐	☐	☐	☐	☐	☐	☐	☐	☐	☐
			☐	☐	☐	☐	☐	☐	☐	☐	☐	☐	☐	☐
			☐	☐	☐	☐	☐	☐	☐	☐	☐	☐	☐	☐
			☐	☐	☐	☐	☐	☐	☐	☐	☐	☐	☐	☐
			☐	☐	☐	☐	☐	☐	☐	☐	☐	☐	☐	☐
			☐	☐	☐	☐	☐	☐	☐	☐	☐	☐	☐	☐
			☐	☐	☐	☐	☐	☐	☐	☐	☐	☐	☐	☐
			☐	☐	☐	☐	☐	☐	☐	☐	☐	☐	☐	☐
			☐	☐	☐	☐	☐	☐	☐	☐	☐	☐	☐	☐
			☐	☐	☐	☐	☐	☐	☐	☐	☐	☐	☐	☐

Notez la date et le titre de l'activité de compréhension écrite que vous venez de faire, puis faites le point sur ce que vous êtes capable de faire.
Vous pourrez ainsi mesurer vos progrès tout au long de l'année et vous situer par rapport au niveau B1.

Compréhension de l'écrit B1			Je peux comprendre l'essentiel de la narration, reconnaître les points significatifs d'un article de presse.			Je peux deviner, à l'aide du contexte, le sens de certains mots inconnus.			Je peux comprendre les descriptions de sentiments ou de souhaits.			Je peux distinguer l'idée essentielle des détails et identifier la principale conclusion de l'argumentation.		
Date	Titre de l'activité du manuel ou du fichier de l'élève	Page	☺	😐	☹	☺	😐	☹	☺	😐	☹	☺	😐	☹
			☐	☐	☐	☐	☐	☐	☐	☐	☐	☐	☐	☐
			☐	☐	☐	☐	☐	☐	☐	☐	☐	☐	☐	☐
			☐	☐	☐	☐	☐	☐	☐	☐	☐	☐	☐	☐
			☐	☐	☐	☐	☐	☐	☐	☐	☐	☐	☐	☐
			☐	☐	☐	☐	☐	☐	☐	☐	☐	☐	☐	☐
			☐	☐	☐	☐	☐	☐	☐	☐	☐	☐	☐	☐
			☐	☐	☐	☐	☐	☐	☐	☐	☐	☐	☐	☐
			☐	☐	☐	☐	☐	☐	☐	☐	☐	☐	☐	☐
			☐	☐	☐	☐	☐	☐	☐	☐	☐	☐	☐	☐
			☐	☐	☐	☐	☐	☐	☐	☐	☐	☐	☐	☐
			☐	☐	☐	☐	☐	☐	☐	☐	☐	☐	☐	☐

Notez la date et le titre de l'activité d'expression orale en continu que vous venez de faire, puis faites le point sur ce que vous êtes capable de faire. Vous pourrez ainsi mesurer vos progrès tout au long de l'année et vous situer par rapport au niveau B1.

Expression orale en continu B1			**Je peux raconter une histoire, l'intrigue d'un film, rendre compte d'un événement réel ou imaginaire.**			**Je peux faire un exposé simple que j'ai préparé et développer les points importants avec précision.**			**Je peux expliquer mes opinions en donnant des arguments, décrire mes sentiments et mes réactions.**			**Je peux parler de manière compréhensible et sans trop hésiter, même si je fais des pauses pour réfléchir.**		
Date	**Titre de l'activité du manuel ou du fichier de l'élève**	**Page**	☺	😐	☹	☺	😐	☹	☺	😐	☹	☺	😐	☹
			☐	☐	☐	☐	☐	☐	☐	☐	☐	☐	☐	☐
			☐	☐	☐	☐	☐	☐	☐	☐	☐	☐	☐	☐
			☐	☐	☐	☐	☐	☐	☐	☐	☐	☐	☐	☐
			☐	☐	☐	☐	☐	☐	☐	☐	☐	☐	☐	☐
			☐	☐	☐	☐	☐	☐	☐	☐	☐	☐	☐	☐
			☐	☐	☐	☐	☐	☐	☐	☐	☐	☐	☐	☐
			☐	☐	☐	☐	☐	☐	☐	☐	☐	☐	☐	☐
			☐	☐	☐	☐	☐	☐	☐	☐	☐	☐	☐	☐
			☐	☐	☐	☐	☐	☐	☐	☐	☐	☐	☐	☐
			☐	☐	☐	☐	☐	☐	☐	☐	☐	☐	☐	☐
			☐	☐	☐	☐	☐	☐	☐	☐	☐	☐	☐	☐

Notez la date et le titre de l'activité d'interaction orale que vous venez de faire, puis faites le point sur ce que vous êtes capable de faire.
Vous pourrez ainsi mesurer vos progrès tout au long de l'année et vous situer par rapport au niveau B1.

Interaction orale B1			Je peux participer activement et sans préparation à une discussion sur un thème familier, même si je dois parfois chercher mes mots.			Je peux interviewer quelqu'un sur un sujet précis si j'ai préparé le questionnaire et poser des questions spontanées.			Je peux, sans préparation, justifier brièvement mes opinions ou mes actes, et expliquer pourquoi je suis en désaccord avec un point de vue qui a été exprimé.			Je peux interrompre poliment mon interlocuteur et m'exprimer autrement s'il ne me comprend pas.		
Date	**Titre de l'activité du manuel ou du fichier de l'élève**	**Page**	☺	😐	☹	☺	😐	☹	☺	😐	☹	☺	😐	☹
			☐	☐	☐	☐	☐	☐	☐	☐	☐	☐	☐	☐
			☐	☐	☐	☐	☐	☐	☐	☐	☐	☐	☐	☐
			☐	☐	☐	☐	☐	☐	☐	☐	☐	☐	☐	☐
			☐	☐	☐	☐	☐	☐	☐	☐	☐	☐	☐	☐
			☐	☐	☐	☐	☐	☐	☐	☐	☐	☐	☐	☐
			☐	☐	☐	☐	☐	☐	☐	☐	☐	☐	☐	☐
			☐	☐	☐	☐	☐	☐	☐	☐	☐	☐	☐	☐
			☐	☐	☐	☐	☐	☐	☐	☐	☐	☐	☐	☐
			☐	☐	☐	☐	☐	☐	☐	☐	☐	☐	☐	☐
			☐	☐	☐	☐	☐	☐	☐	☐	☐	☐	☐	☐
			☐	☐	☐	☐	☐	☐	☐	☐	☐	☐	☐	☐

Notez la date et le titre de l'activité d'expression écrite que vous venez de faire, puis faites le point sur ce que vous êtes capable de faire.
Vous pourrez ainsi mesurer vos progrès tout au long de l'année et vous situer par rapport au niveau B1.

Expression écrite B1			Je peux décrire un événement, raconter une histoire, faire le compte-rendu d'un film, en mettant en relief la succession et la cohérence des événements et des comportements.			Je peux écrire sur un sujet familier et structurer mon texte en utilisant des mots de liaison variés.			Je peux exposer mes goûts, exprimer un point de vue personnel sans utiliser trop souvent le dictionnaire.			Je peux supprimer en me relisant les erreurs de langue les plus importantes.		
Date	**Titre de l'activité du manuel ou du fichier de l'élève**	**Page**	☺	😐	☹	☺	😐	☹	☺	😐	☹	☺	😐	☹
			☐	☐	☐	☐	☐	☐	☐	☐	☐	☐	☐	☐
			☐	☐	☐	☐	☐	☐	☐	☐	☐	☐	☐	☐
			☐	☐	☐	☐	☐	☐	☐	☐	☐	☐	☐	☐
			☐	☐	☐	☐	☐	☐	☐	☐	☐	☐	☐	☐
			☐	☐	☐	☐	☐	☐	☐	☐	☐	☐	☐	☐
			☐	☐	☐	☐	☐	☐	☐	☐	☐	☐	☐	☐
			☐	☐	☐	☐	☐	☐	☐	☐	☐	☐	☐	☐
			☐	☐	☐	☐	☐	☐	☐	☐	☐	☐	☐	☐
			☐	☐	☐	☐	☐	☐	☐	☐	☐	☐	☐	☐
			☐	☐	☐	☐	☐	☐	☐	☐	☐	☐	☐	☐
			☐	☐	☐	☐	☐	☐	☐	☐	☐	☐	☐	☐

N° d'éditeur 10245866 - Dépôt légal : juin 2017
N° d'impression : 1801713 - Imprimé en France par Normandie Roto Impression s.a.s. à Lonrai (Orne)